Stravinsky: *The Rite of Spring*

CAMBRIDGE MUSIC HANDBOOKS

GENERAL EDITOR   Julian Rushton

Recent titles

Bach: *The Brandenburg Concertos*   MALCOLM BOYD
Bartók: *Concerto for Orchestra*   DAVID COOPER
Beethoven: *Eroica Symphony*   THOMAS SIPE
Beethoven: *Pastoral Symphony*   DAVID WYN JONES
Beethoven: The 'Moonlight' and other Sonatas, Op. 27
   and Op. 31   TIMOTHY JONES
Beethoven: Symphony No. 9   NICHOLAS COOK
Beethoven: Violin Concerto   ROBIN STOWELL
Berlioz: *Roméo et Juliette*   JULIAN RUSHTON
Brahms: Clarinet Quintet   COLIN LAWSON
Brahms: *A German Requiem*   MICHAEL MUSGRAVE
Brahms: Symphony No. 1   DAVID BRODBECK
Britten: *War Requiem*   MERVYN COOKE
Bruckner: Symphony No. 8   BENJAMIN M. KORSTVEDT
Chopin: The Piano Concertos   JOHN RINK
Debussy: *La mer*   SIMON TREZISE
Dowland: Lachrimae (1604)   PETER HOLMAN
Dvořák: Cello Concerto   JAN SMAZNY
Elgar: *'Enigma' Variations*   JULIAN RUSHTON
Gershwin: *Rhapsody in Blue*   DAVID SCHIFF
Haydn: The 'Paris' Symphonies   BERNARD HARRISON
Haydn: String Quartets, Op. 50   W. DEAN SUTCLIFFE
Holst: *The Planets*   RICHARD GREENE
Ives: *Concord Sonata*   GEOFFREY BLOCK
Liszt: Sonata in B Minor   KENNETH HAMILTON
Mahler: *Das Lied von der Erde*   STEPHEN E. HEFLING
Mahler: Symphony No. 3   PETER FRANKLIN
Mendelssohn: *The Hebrides* and other overtures   R. LARRY TODD
Messiaen: *Quatuor pour la fin du Temps*   ANTHONY POPLE
Monteverdi: Vespers (1610)   JOHN WHENHAM
Mozart: Clarinet Concerto   COLIN LAWSON
Mozart: The 'Haydn' Quartets   JOHN IRVING
Mozart: The 'Jupiter' Symphony   ELAINE R. SISMAN
Mozart: Piano Concertos Nos. 20 and 21   DAVIS GRAYSON
Nielsen: Symphony No. 5   DAVID FANNING
Sibelius: Symphony No. 5   JAMES HEPOKOSKI
Strauss: *Also sprach Zarathustra*   JOHN WILLIAMSON
Stravinsky: *The Rite of Spring*   PETER HILL
The Beatles: *Sgt. Pepper's Lonely Hearts Club Band*   ALLAN MOORE
Tippett: *A Child of our Time*   KENNETH GLOAG
Verdi: Requiem   DAVID ROSEN
Vivaldi: *The Four Seasons* and other concertos, Op. 8   PAUL EVERETT

Stravinsky: *The Rite of Spring*

Peter Hill

CAMBRIDGE UNIVERSITY PRESS
Cambridge, New York, Melbourne, Madrid, Cape Town, Singapore, São Paulo

Cambridge University Press
The Edinburgh Building, Cambridge CB2 2RU, UK

Published in the United States of America by Cambridge University Press, New York

www.cambridge.org
Information on this title: www.cambridge.org/9780521622219

First published 2000
Reprinted 2004

A catalogue record for this publication is available from the British Library

Library of Congress Cataloguing in Publication data
Hill, Peter, 1948–
Stravinsky: The rite of spring / Peter Hill.
p.   cm. (Cambridge music handbooks)
Includes bibliographical references and discography.
ISBN 0 521 62221 2 (hardback)   ISBN 0 521 62714 1 (paperback). Stravinsky, Igor,
1882–1971. Vesna svëishchennaëi. I. Title: Rite of spring. II. Title.
III. Series.
ML410.S932 H55 2000
784.2'1556 – dc21   00-023703

ISBN-13   978-0-521-62221-9 hardback
ISBN-10   0-521-62221-2 hardback

ISBN-13   978-0-521-62714-6 paperback
ISBN-10   0-521-62714-1 paperback

Transferred to digital printing 2005

Contents

Preface

For many people the *Rite of Spring* is the first masterpiece of the twentieth century to break completely with the past. The paradox is that it is also a work more deeply rooted in tradition than any other Stravinsky composed. The music is based on a scenario devised by Stravinsky with Nikolai Roerich – artist, archaeologist and expert on folk art and customs. The seriousness with which they approached their task resulted in a work unique in Stravinsky's output for the absence of irony or theatrical artifice. The *Rite* is third in the trio of ballets which Stravinsky composed for Diaghilev's *Ballets Russes* between 1910 and 1913. The scandal attending the *Rite*'s première on 29 May 1913 became legendary: it also marked Stravinsky for life. Partly because it was so controversial, the *Rite* is surrounded by anecdote, myth and hearsay through which the historian must sift, aware that much is contradictory or otherwise unreliable. Much of the problem stems from Stravinsky himself, who tried in later years to distance the music from its dramatic origins. The story of how and why he did this is recounted in Part III of this book, 'Aftermath'.

Before Stravinsky's death in 1971, the composer's own memoirs naturally dominated discussion. Since then a radical reappraisal has gathered momentum. Heading the list of significant publications are a number by Robert Craft, who acted as Stravinsky's assistant from 1949 onwards; there are also the books devoted to the *Rite* by Allen Forte and by Pieter van den Toorn, which attempt from different viewpoints a detailed explanation of its language, or at least of its 'vocabulary'. Two events have added greatly to our knowledge of the *Rite*. The first, which took place in Stravinsky's lifetime, in 1969, was the publication of the sketches together with notes on the choreography; the other was the discovery by Lawrence Morton (in 1979) of the extent to which the *Rite* is based on folk music borrowings. More recently Richard Taruskin, epitomising the revisionary approach of recent writings, has stressed the paradox in the *Rite*, seeing Stravinsky's most revolutionary early work as rooted in Russian traditions, a fusion of extremes of old and new. Largely this is a matter of the thoroughness with which Stravinsky and Roerich attempted an authentic embodiment of Stravinsky's initial vision of ritual sacrifice; but it concerns also Stravinsky's debt (never properly acknowledged in his own writings) to his teacher, Rimsky-Korsakov.

The *Rite* is universally viewed as an icon of modernism, dominating the twentieth century as Beethoven's Ninth Symphony did the nineteenth. For this reason it has been regularly commandeered by pressure groups. In the early days it was exploited by critics, both for and against; later by avant-garde composers, and later still by analysts and historians, so that the actual music of the *Rite* all but disappears in the welter of grinding axes. Like other writers I am interested in why the *Rite* is as it is; but unlike them my answers come largely from within the music itself.

Nonetheless, any discussion of Stravinsky's music must never forget the simple truth that the *Rite* is a dramatic work; however effective as a concert item, the form in which it is best known, the *Rite* was conceived and composed as a ballet. Stravinsky's dramatic instincts were formed in childhood, as the son of a famous father, Fyodor, who had a glittering career as a bass soloist at the Mariinsky Theatre in St Petersburg. Stravinsky *père* was admired for the psychological insight of his portrayals and his mastery of every aspect of stagecraft. Igor Stravinsky studied with Rimsky-Korsakov, the composer of no fewer than fifteen operas, and the older man became, in effect, a second father to Stravinsky after Fyodor's death in 1902. Finally, Stravinsky received a further theatrical education at the hands of the impresario Diaghilev, the artist Benois and the choreographer Fokine, with whom he worked on *Firebird* and *Petrushka*. The greatest paradox of Stravinsky's life is that, despite his strident mid-career assertion of the autonomous nature of music, Stravinsky's musical output remained essentially theatrical.

The book divides into three. The first part (Chapters 1–3) deals with the *Rite*'s inception, composition and the steps towards the first performance. The account of the rehearsals for the original production acts as a prelude to the second section, the detailed commentary on the music (Chapters 4–5).

The third section examines aspects of the *Rite*'s history since the date of its notorious première, 29 May 1913. There is a short anthology of important texts about the *Rite* as well as interesting (or entertaining) anecdotes and a section on recordings from the earliest (in the 1920s) to the present day, including those by Stravinsky. In between, I examine the apparent repudiation by Stravinsky of his original ideas for the *Rite* and piece together something of the true picture which Stravinsky at various times in his life seems to have been at pains to conceal.

With so much about the *Rite* in print I might have set out to write a guide to the existing literature. I decided from the outset against this, and though greatly indebted to the research of others – the writings of Craft and Taruskin, in particular, have been constant companions – the approach and conclusions are very much my own. My other decision was to try to write about the music in a way that avoided what Stravinsky called 'useless generalities' without on the other hand overwhelming the reader with technical detail. In this I have been greatly helped by the generous provision of music examples allowed by the publisher; my thanks also to Boosey and Hawkes for the necessary permissions and for allowing me to reproduce pages from the volume of sketches.

A number of individuals gave valuable advice and encouragement, among them Philip Carleston, Eric Clarke, Edward Garden, Malcolm MacDonald, Rosamund McGuinness, George Nicholson, David Patmore and Douglas Young. I also owe a debt (greater than he can imagine) to my inspired duo-partner, Ben Frith, veteran with me of countless performances of Stravinsky's four-hand arrangement of the *Rite*. Julian Rushton, the series editor, deciphered my early drafts and his shrewd comments greatly helped me to clarify my intentions. Thanks also go to Penny Souster and her colleagues at Cambridge University Press for dealing so efficiently with what is at times quite a complicated book, and to the copy-editor, Linda Woodward, for numerous improvements and for so deftly eliminating inconsistencies and infelicities, and for answering all queries by return. My special thanks go to three people each of whom generously put their expertise at my disposal: Tim Day, of the National Sound Archive, Nigel Simeone, who loaned me a vast amount of material of which I was unaware, and Colin

Roth who not only guided me through the intrigues of the *Ballets Russes* but applied his brilliant editorial skills to my typescript. Lastly my very special gratitude to my wife, Charlotte, both for tolerating my obsession with the subject ('living with Igor', as my children put it) and for many apparently casual comments which proved on reflection to contain searching insights.

PETER HILL, *Sheffield, January 2000*

Part I

Prelude

1

Origins

The idea of *Le Sacre du printemps* came to me while I was still composing
The Firebird. I had dreamed a scene of pagan ritual in which a chosen
sacrificial virgin danced herself to death. This vision was not accompanied
by concrete musical ideas, however . . .[1]

So runs Stravinsky's last and best-known account of his first inspiration
for the *Rite*. There are, however, at least four others from earlier in his
life, each of which has features which are unique. One of the earliest of
these directly contradicts the legend of the *Rite*'s conception which
Stravinsky later chose to foster. It comes in an article by Stravinsky
written to coincide with the *Rite*'s first revival, in 1920, in a new
production with supposedly abstract choreography by Massine. Hence
Stravinsky was at pains to stress that the pagan setting of the original
production had been secondary to purely musical ideas. Since these were
in a 'strong and brutal manner, as a point of departure I used the very
image evoked by the music. Being a Russian, for me this image took
form as the epoch of prehistoric Russia. But bear in mind that the idea
came from the music and not the music from the idea'.[2]

The earliest of Stravinsky's accounts, dating from 1912, is the
simplest:[3] a 'first thought' which 'came to me as I was finishing *The
Firebird*, spring 1910'. What the 'thought' was Stravinsky does not say,
but in 1931 in the biography by André Schaeffner, based largely on
conversations with Stravinsky, this had become a 'dream' – 'A ballet
unfolded, consisting of a single dance, danced to the point of exhaustion, of a young girl before a group of elders of fabulous age, desiccated
almost to petrifaction.'[4] Four years later, in Stravinsky's autobiography,
the dream is a 'fleeting vision' – 'I saw in imagination a solemn pagan
rite: sage elders, seated in a circle, watched a young girl dance herself

to death. They were sacrificing her to propitiate the god of spring.'[5]

Thought, vision, dream – it hardly matters, though it is worth noting how often in Stravinsky's life he had such premonitions (*L'Histoire du Soldat* and the Octet are notable examples).[6] The discrepancies suggest that Stravinsky's memoirs need to be treated with caution.[7] Nonetheless the progression between the second and third of these accounts may well describe the evolution of Stravinsky's ideas in 1910 – the dancer's exhaustion becomes her death, this in turn leads to the idea of human sacrifice, and so to a setting in pagan prehistory. And the best evidence that, details apart, this is the true version of events – that the idea of the ballet did indeed come to Stravinsky before the music – is the fact that he at once turned for help to Nikolai Roerich, Russia's leading expert in folk art and ancient ritual. As Stravinsky put it in his first account of the ballet's conception, 'who else could help me, who else knows the secret of our ancestors' close feeling for the earth?'[8]

Stravinsky moved fast. Already only two months later, by the time he left for Paris in May to attend rehearsals of *The Firebird*, he and Roerich had met, had decided on a title – 'The Great Sacrifice' – and a libretto was in existence together with a sheet of musical sketches. So much is clear from the earliest letter in the Stravinsky–Roerich correspondence to have survived.[9] It was written in haste from Stravinsky's home at Ustilug whence he had returned, a week after *The Firebird*'s première (25 June 1910), in order to bring his family to Paris so that his wife, Catherine, could enjoy at first hand the ballet's triumph (the Paris run had been extended after planned performances in London had been cancelled on the death of Edward VII on 6 May).[10] Stravinsky's letter has a faintly deferential tone. Its main purpose seems to have been to reassure Roerich of Stravinsky's credentials by dwelling on the details of *The Firebird*'s reception – before this triumph Stravinsky's standing as a composer had been negligible.

The correspondence makes clear the value Stravinsky placed on Roerich's participation. Roerich was a rare blend of scholar with artist and visionary. He began his career as an archaeologist, training as a painter at the St Petersburg Academy, and his subsequent prolific output was rooted in his studies in anthropology and archaeology. Benois remembered him as 'utterly absorbed in dreams of prehistoric, patriarchal and religious life – of the days when the vast, limitless plains of Russia and the shores of her lakes and rivers were peopled with the forefathers of the present inhabitants. Roerich's mystic, spiritual experiences made him strangely susceptible to the charm of the ancient world. He felt in it something primordial and weird, something that is intimately linked with nature – with that Northern nature he adored, the inspiration of his finest pictures'.[11] *The Forefathers* was painted in 1911, precisely at the time of Roerich's collaboration with Stravinsky. The picture might almost be a sketch for the opening of the *Rite*, whose early pages quiver with the sound of *dudki* (pipes). Here, Orpheus-like, primitive man charms with his piping a circle of wild beasts, in this case bears, reflecting the Slavic tradition that bears were man's forefathers.[12]

One reason for Stravinsky's approach to Roerich must have been the success of his famously austere designs[13] for Act 2 of Borodin's *Prince Igor*, produced as part of Diaghilev's *Saison Russe* in Paris in 1909. Although Stravinsky cannot have seen the production he must have been aware of the sensation they created – 'an empty, desolate landscape, in which are pitched the beehive tents of the Polovtsi, and the smoke of their camp-fires rises against a tawny sky. The Parisian audience have the strange sensation of being transported to the ends of the earth'.[14]

Roerich must have received the approach from Stravinsky with a strong sense of destiny. The previous year Roerich had published 'Joy in Art', a lengthy essay whose climax Richard Taruskin calls 'a lyrical Neolithic fantasy'.[15] A passage from this describes the springtime festivities – 'A holiday. Let it be the one with which the victory of the springtime sun was always celebrated. When all went out into the woods for long stretches of time to admire the fragrance of the trees: when they made fragrant wreaths out of the early greenery, and adorned themselves with them. When swift dances were danced . . . When horns and pipes of bone and wood were played . . .'[16]

The resemblance to the *Rite* gives some support to Roerich's later claim that the idea for the *Rite* was entirely his and had nothing to do with Stravinsky. According to this version of events, it was Diaghilev who had the idea of teaming Roerich with his new discovery, Stravinsky.[17] Roerich then offered Stravinsky two ready-made scenarios – 'A Game of Chess' and 'The Great Sacrifice' – Stravinsky choosing the latter.[18] However, the correspondence between Stravinsky and Roerich, in which it is clear that the new ballet was for the time being to be a secret from Diaghilev, proves otherwise.[19] When, in the aftermath of the success of *The Firebird*, Diaghilev approached Stravinsky with the idea of a ballet based on Poe's *The Mask of the Red Death*, Stravinsky had to admit that he had another project in view. Diaghilev, scenting disloyalty, was so enraged that Stravinsky was forced to admit the details of the new ballet; fortunately, Diaghilev's reaction to the proposal was one of delight.[20] The likely explanation for the discrepancies between the accounts by Roerich and Stravinsky is that the composer's vision of human sacrifice was indeed the spark, while the details of the festivities to which the sacrifice would be the climax came from Roerich.[21]

Having revealed his plans for the new ballet to Diaghilev and received his encouragement, Stravinsky was impatient to begin work. Writing to Roerich from La Baule in Brittany, Stravinsky reveals that he has started making sketches for the music even while still waiting to receive from Roerich the two versions of the ballet's libretto. He asks, 'Have you done anything for it yet?' a reference to Roerich's projected designs for the sets and costumes.[22]

In the event 'our child' (as Stravinsky called the ballet in his letters to Roerich) had to wait another year for, as Stravinsky describes in his autobiography, he was unexpectedly side-tracked. 'Before tackling the *Sacre du Printemps*, which would be a long and difficult task, I wanted to refresh myself by composing an orchestral piece in which the piano would play the most important part ... I had in mind a distinct picture of a puppet, suddenly endowed with life, exasperating the patience of the orchestra with diabolical cascades of arpeggios.'[23] Initially conceived as a *Pièce Burlesque*,[24] the idea rapidly took shape in Stravinsky's mind for a dramatic work, with the maverick piano part representing the Russian folk puppet, Petrushka. Thus it was that when Diaghilev and Nijinsky visited Stravinsky in Lausanne at the end of September 1910 expecting to hear work in progress on the *Rite*, they heard instead Stravinsky play this new composition, which he called 'Petrushka's Cry'.[25]

For almost exactly a year – the year of *Petrushka* – the Stravinsky–Roerich correspondence ceases, their only contact being a message via Benois (in a letter dated 3 November 1910) with an apology for interrupting their work and an excuse – 'I'd never be able to have "The Great Sacrifice" ready by April, which was the deadline Diaghilev set ...'[26] But by July the following year Stravinsky, now back in Russia at his home in Ustilug, was impatient to recommence. 'I feel it is imperative that we see each other to decide about every detail – especially every question of staging...'[27] Roerich, however, was hard at work with another project. He had designed (in neo-Russian style) the church on the estate of his patron Princess Tenisheva at Talashkino (near Smolensk) and was now executing interior and exterior murals and mosaics – the painting discussed earlier (*The Forefathers*) is a study for the mosaic over the church's main entrance. So there was nothing for it but to go to Talashkino, a trip which proved unexpectedly hazardous as well as inconvenient: in order to expedite the journey Stravinsky travelled the section from Brest-Litovsk to Smolensk in a cattle car in which he found himself penned in with a none-too-friendly bull.[28]

There is something so apt about Talashkino as the birthplace of the *Rite* that the place and its formidable owner deserve a digression. The Princess was a passionate admirer of Russian folk art, and had founded a wood-carving workshop on the lines of the museum and workshops at Abramtsevo founded in the 1870s by the railway tycoon Savva Mamontov.[29] Despite or perhaps because of their common interest, relations between the two were strained: the Princess regarded the products of Abramtsevo as unimaginative. Moreover the Princess harboured a grudge: as a singer she had been rejected in 1885 on auditioning for Mamontov's opera company.[30] Nonetheless the two had agreed jointly to sponsor Diaghilev's *World of Art* magazine (the first issue appeared in 1898) on the understanding, largely unfulfilled, that the magazine would emphasise crafts and industrial design.[31] Relations between the Princess and Diaghilev, always uneasy, finally foundered in 1903 when she failed to persuade Diaghilev to appoint Roerich as editor in place of Benois. The magazine closed the following year.

In the propitious surroundings of Talashkino work on the *Rite* prospered and within a few days, as Stravinsky later recalled, the plan of action and titles of the dances had been decided. Roerich began work on the designs, sketching backdrops and seeking inspiration in the Princess's collection for his costume designs.[32] No documents have survived from the meeting, but a few months before the première Stravinsky enclosed a summary of the libretto in a letter to Nikolai Findeyzen, editor of the *Russian Musical Gazette*.

In a few days we worked out the libretto which – roughly – follows. 'The name of the *First Part* is *The Kiss of the Earth*. It contains the ancient Slavic games, "The Joy of Spring." Orchestral introduction: a swarm of spring pipes [*dudki*]. Then after the curtain rises, fortunetelling; Khorovod (ritual games of dancing in a ring); a Khorovod game ending in exhaustion; Khorovod games between two villages. All of this is interrupted by the procession of "The Old Wise Man", who kisses the earth. The first part ends in a frenzied dance of the people drunk with spring.

Part Two. The secret night-games of the maidens on the sacred hill. One of them is consecrated for the sacrificial offering. She enters a stone labyrinth while the other maidens glorify her in a wild, martial dance. Then the "Old Wise Men" arrive, and the chosen one is left alone with them. She dances her last "Sacred Dance", The Great Offering, which is the title of the *Second Part*. The Old Wise Men witness this last dance, which ends with the death of the chosen one.'[33]

The next account by Stravinsky was the much more detailed résumé published in the avant-garde journal *Montjoie!* on the very day of the *Rite*'s first performance, 29 May 1913. This fascinating document – hotly disputed by Stravinsky who condemned it as a travesty despite overwhelming evidence that he was its author – adds many vivid details.[34] The first scene features a woman of immense age 'who knows the secrets of nature and who teaches her sons Divination... The adolescent boys beside her are the Augurs of Spring who mark with their steps, on the spot, the rhythm of spring'. The games become war-like as the groups 'separate and enter into combat, messengers going from one to another, quarrelling'. In Part II the stone labyrinth is replaced by the marking out of a circle within which the Chosen One will be confined. Finally as she dances her Sacrificial Dance the Ancestors perceive her exhaustion and 'glide towards her like rapacious monsters, so that she may not touch the ground in falling; they raise her and hold her towards the sky...'[35]

Finally there is the programme note written by Stravinsky at the request of the conductor Koussevitzky for the first Russian concert performance of the *Rite* (18 February 1914). In this we learn two further details which are clearly reflected in Stravinsky's score. Besides the old woman and the adolescent boys the first scene is overlooked by celebrants seated on hills who blow *dudki*. Later the choosing of the maiden is made more specific than in earlier accounts – 'Fate points to her twice: twice she is caught in one of the circles without an exit'[36] – fateful moments pinpointed by the stinging tocsins[37] for muted horns and trumpets which interrupt the maidens' round dance.

2

Sketches

We turn now to the sketches for the *Rite*, one of the most extraordinary documents in musical history, and sufficiently complete for us to reconstruct, almost step by step, the act of composition.[1]

The sketches have passed through the hands of a number of owners. Originally they belonged to Misia Sert who had been given them by Stravinsky. She in turn presented them to Diaghilev who hoped to sell them to raise money in order to finance the *Rite*'s second production, in 1920, and to this end asked Stravinsky to autograph them: hence the inscription on the first sheet – 'Seriozhe Diaghilev, these sketches of the 'Spring' from his great friend Igor, Paris, Oct. 1920.' They were subsequently owned by Boris Kochno,[2] and were then acquired in 1963 by André Meyer.

In 1969 the sketches were published by Boosey and Hawkes in a handsome facsimile.[3] The quality of reproduction is such that one can distinguish clearly between pen and pencil, and thanks to the use of colour, between emendations in neat red ink or scrawled blue pencil. Throughout, Stravinsky's handwriting is marvellously expressive, ranging from the strong clear hand of his fair copies to feverish scribbles, such as the page on which he records the first inspiration for the 'Glorification of the Chosen One', the slashes of his pencil stabbing out the rhythms of the music (Ex. 2.1).

As one would expect, the sketches give a fascinating insight into Stravinsky's working methods at the time. Even more valuably they reveal a conception which in some respects is startlingly different from the finished score. The shadowy presence of these other possibilities is like an X-ray of a familiar painting, so familiar that the finished work seems inevitable: we simply accept and do not notice the *Rite*'s oddities. How often, for example, do listeners wonder why towards the end of

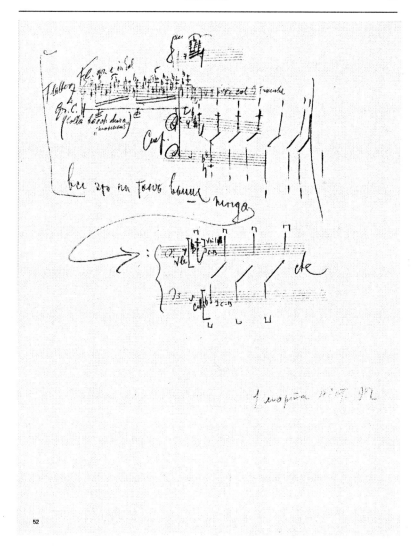

Ex. 2.1 Glorification of the Chosen One (Sketches, p. 52)

'Augurs of Spring' (fig. 28 + 5) we hear what will become the tune of 'Spring Rounds'? It is clear from the sketches that Stravinsky intended 'Spring Rounds' (rather than 'Ritual of Abduction', as in the finished score) to follow 'Augurs': the addition of the broad melody from 'Spring

Rounds' to the climax of 'Augurs' was presumably intended as an overlap joining the two sections. What then happened is a striking illustration of the way Stravinsky's mind worked. Reluctant as ever to waste anything, Stravinsky retained rather than deleted the now redundant transition: after all, he might have argued, the music still makes a point, casting a shadow over a passage (the music of the 'Young Girls', starting with the horn solo at fig. 25) which has come as close as anything in the *Rite* to being tranquil. He adds a second transition (the tutti from fig. 31), this time aiming towards 'Ritual of Abduction'. Something further is then needed to bridge the two transitions: and this explains the rising sequences, which accomplish the task with (it has to be said) a fairly obvious cranking through the gears (figs. 31–2). True to form the material which fills this gap is already in existence. We find it in a stray figure (a derivative of the D♭ B♭ E♭ B♭ ostinato) which at the time he jotted it down Stravinsky was uncertain how to use;[4] at the same time he gives new life to yet another existing idea, the pattern of syncopations from the hammered repeated chords which open 'Augurs' (fig. 13). This tendency of Stravinsky to borrow from himself is one reason for the myriad cross-references which flicker through Part I.

Here then is Stravinsky at work, flexible and pragmatic in deciding on a major change in architecture; yet when it comes to detail he is like a parsimonious chef, every scrap somehow finding a place in the pot. Consistent with this is the almost complete absence of pre-compositional working. Everything sketched by Stravinsky is a concrete musical idea, in almost every case clearly identifiable with the finished work. There are two important exceptions. One is the copying down of folk melodies, and the other comes when Stravinsky begins work on the 'Introduction' to Part II, when he carefully copied a chord sequence already used in the 'Sacrificial Dance'.[5] Both will be discussed later. Though to say so goes against the grain of recent Stravinsky research, with its sceptical scrutiny of all his later comments, the sketches for the *Rite* do support his famous remark – 'I was guided by no system . . . I had only my ear to help me.'[6]

For the most part Stravinsky steps straight from brief, unformed jottings to a fluent draft, with little or no intermediary working. Sometimes the explanation may be that one or more sheets is missing.

Alternatively, it seems probable that much of the detailed working out was never committed to paper because it was done by Stravinsky at the piano, as was his habit. Later he would recall the tiny room, eight foot square, in the pension at Clarens where much of the *Rite* was composed, 'whose only furniture was a small upright piano which I kept muted (I always work at a muted piano), a table, and two chairs'.[7] The piano seems to have exerted an unseen influence on the *Rite*, far more than just a useful composing tool. The music has strong pianistic qualities: the snug 'fit' under the pianist's hands of its harmonies suggests that many were discovered while improvising. Then there is the left hand/right hand 'vamp' which features so strongly in Part II (in 'Glorification of the Chosen One' and 'Sacrificial Dance') and which is surely pianistic in origin; the cartoon by Cocteau of Stravinsky rehearsing the *Rite* shows him making just such a gesture, his right hand exaggeratedly raised the better to pound the keys.

Stravinsky found time to make a two-hand piano version for rehearsals (now lost),[8] as well as the magnificent four-hand arrangement, the first version of the *Rite* to be published, in May 1913. It was this version – or, to be exact, the first half of it – that Debussy and Stravinsky played through on 9 June 1912.[9] Heard in concert the four-hand version makes a distinctive and valid alternative: pared to essentials the music's rhythmic and harmonic dissonance have an even sharper focus. The effect of the piano version is strikingly prophetic in view of the later direction of Stravinsky's music, foreshadowing, for example, the instrumentation of *Les Noces*.

Evidence comes in the very first sheet that much that would otherwise have been written down was retained by Stravinsky in his fingers. Devoted to the opening of 'Augurs', this begins with fragments, in two of which we can discern progress towards the electrifying harmony which accompanies the first action on stage (fig. 13). The upper notes of the 'right hand' chord are in place an octave higher, in the form of the ostinato (initially given in reverse, as E♭ B♭ D♭ B♭ etc.); against this Stravinsky tries first arpeggios of E minor (spelled with a C♭) and C, then an E arpeggio with a G♯. Astonishingly, immediately below these on the same sheet, is the beginning of a continuity draft which, racing ahead fluently over two further sheets, takes the music from the opening chords (at fig. 13) right up to the explosive *cæsura* (before fig. 22) and beyond into the subsequent transition (Ex. 2.2). The probable explanation is that the intermediate stage, involving the crucial step of transferring the Eb7/E harmony to its thick bass sonority, must have been discovered at the piano. It is easy to imagine Stravinsky then using the piano to work out the structure of 'Augurs', with the hammered repetitions framing episodes drawn from fragments from the top half of the first sheet.

We are so accustomed to accounts of the *Rite* which treat it as 'pure' or abstract music that we ignore just how much the course of the music runs hand in hand with events on stage. The music opens with antiphonal exchanges between the strings – the famous hammered chords, the adolescents tapping out the 'rhythm of Spring'[10] – and woodwind: these are the pipe-playing celebrants, the image of these *dudki* having already been developed in the 'Introduction' with its ecstatic medley of woodwind solos. The old woman is identified with the peremptory chords at fig. 15 – see Ex. 2.3a, and the first entry in Ex. 2.2 which is a tone lower than the final score.[11] As the antiphonal exchanges continue, the old woman ('half woman, half beast'[12]) acquires a syncopated or hobbling motif. Interestingly, Stravinsky's sketches show that he envisaged this in semiquavers at first – the handwriting is curious, as though Stravinsky had devised the rhythm before finding a tune to fit it – in line with the description he gave to Roerich of the old woman: 'She is constantly before my eyes as I compose . . . I see her running in front of the group, stopping them sometimes, and interrupting the rhythmic flow.'[13] See Ex. 2.3b and Ex. 2.2.

The second phase begins, after a *fortissimo cæsura* (before fig. 22) with the transition which Stravinsky described to Roerich in the same letter: 'I have connected – a smooth jointure with which I am very pleased – the "Dance of the Maidens" and the "Divination With Twigs."'[14]

Three weeks after beginning work, writing to Roerich, Stravinsky conveys his elation. 'I have already begun to compose, and have sketched the Introduction for *dudki*, and the Divination With Twigs in a state of passion and excitement.'[15] Mention of the missing sketches for the 'Introduction' is tantalising. Stravinsky's letter contradicts his later recollection[16] that the 'Introduction' was written only after the rest of Part I. (Was Stravinsky confusing Part I with Part II, whose 'Introduction' was indeed composed last?) Craft supports the later account, on the

Ex. 2.2 Augurs of Spring (Sketches, p. 3)

grounds that to begin at the beginning was not Stravinsky's normal practice. However, by 'Introduction' Stravinsky's letter to Roerich may have meant only the transition immediately before the rise of the curtain, beginning with the famous opening bassoon solo transposed a

Ex. 2.3a and Ex. 2.3b Augurs of Spring: music of the old woman

semitone lower (fig. 12). One fragment of this transition, the pair of chords at fig. 12 + 7, does indeed occur in the first surviving sheet of sketches. More likely the point Stravinsky is making in the letter is that he has extended the idea of *dudki* from the music of 'Augurs' to the 'Introduction': this of course is scored almost entirely for wind soloists.

The sketches for 'Ritual of the Rival Tribes' show how hard Stravinsky worked at the ordering of the material and at measuring the required repetitions. Once sure of the basic ideas he takes stock, assembling his bits and pieces in a lightly sketched 'map'. Its successor[17] is even flimsier in detail, but makes useful advances in structure, for example extending the introductory bar to two bars (as at fig. 57). Yet a third continuity sketch begins again in shorthand, though now with indications of orchestration, and as it proceeds it gathers in more and more detail, for example the sweeping woodwind scales (fig. 57 + 5) were added at this stage. Between each continuity sketch we may imagine Stravinsky working at the piano, gradually kneading his material into shape.

Work proceeded apace, and with such fluency that in the next section to be composed, 'Ritual of Abduction', Stravinsky was so sure of his bearings that he seems to have raced ahead without bothering to make a final continuity draft. 'I have worked very hard', Stravinsky wrote to Benois at the beginning of January, 'and have almost completed the first tableau of *Le Sacre du Printemps* ... if you see Roerich, tell him that I composed very well.'[18] On the same day he began work on the final section of Part I, 'Dance of the Earth', completing it in just five days.

Stravinsky of course was in a hurry, with the première planned for the 1912 season. Then, suddenly and unexpectedly, the pressure was lifted. At this point in the sketches there is a hiatus, with five sheets devoted to another project, *The Nightingale*: very possibly these correspond to the moment when Stravinsky was told of the *Rite*'s postponement.[19] Certainly the decision to postpone cannot have come much later. From 7 January to the beginning of March the sketches contain only two sheets. And for the rest of February Stravinsky was travelling, spending time with the *Ballets Russes* in London and Vienna, which he would hardly have done if working to complete the *Rite* by the spring of 1912.

Stravinsky's last act before interrupting work on the *Rite* was to establish a 'beachhead' (as Craft puts it)[20] into Part II: two ideas which would form the basis of the music of 'Mystic Circles'. The second of these is a development of a two-bar fragment jotted down earlier in among the final sketches for 'Dance of the Earth', and easily recognisable as the 'Mystic Circles' theme at its most intensely chromatic (as at fig. 99).[21]

The first surprise of Part II is that sketches for 'Mystic Circles' far outnumber those for any other section in the *Rite*. How was it that this (in some ways) anachronistic section of the *Rite*,[22] the one closest to *The Firebird*, should have caused Stravinsky so much more trouble than the innovations of 'Glorification of the Chosen One' and 'Dance of the Earth'? One answer is that Stravinsky's opening ideas contain no hint that he was aware of the music's eventual structure. Indeed over the pages to come he works with almost agonising slowness, towards what would eventually be the most evolutionary passage in the *Rite*, the music stealing through the darkness towards the ballet's defining moment, the choosing and glorifying of the Chosen One.

Just how far Stravinsky was from crystallising his ideas can be seen from other jottings in the 'beachhead'. One of these is labelled incorrectly 'For the Amazons', a reference to Stravinsky's earliest conception of the 'Glorification of the Chosen One' as an Amazonian dance, an idea later wisely abandoned 'because of the difficulties of staging cavalry and of introducing so foreign an episode and character'.[23] The true destination of this jerky rhythm will be the eerie climax to Part II's 'Introduction' (figs. 86–9). The others are two entries, both inscribed sideways at the edge of the sheet. In neither case is there any sign that Stravinsky knew how they would be used. One will become the bizarre hip-hop pizzicato which accompanies 'Mystic Circles' at its first entry, the other the passage for two solo cellos which comes just before it.

This was the point at which Stravinsky interrupted his work. Now, as he resumes, a series of dated sheets – commencing on 1 March – chronicle with marvellous precision an astounding burst of creative energy. In the first of these Stravinsky's handwriting explodes from the page as he crams down his first thoughts for 'Glorification', the uprushing anacrusis together with the pianistic 'vamp' (see Ex. 2.1).

Stravinsky did not as yet envisage the long prelude which precedes the rise of the curtain. Part II would have begun with 'Mystic Circles'. This was a long time in reaching its final form, but Stravinsky was clear from the start of its intended effect, leaving a note to himself: 'All this in the clouds, barely audible counterpoint in the strings . . .'[24] The moment when Stravinsky changes his mind is found in a fragment marked 'For the Introduction (Second Tableau)' and recognisable as the music after fig. 86.[25] Quite suddenly Stravinsky seems alive to long-range connections. Here, for example, we find the 'quartal' harmony which is also the harmonic basis of 'Glorification', sketches for which occupy the very next sheet. Stravinsky resumes work on the 'Introduction', with the quartal harmonies now yoked to the jerky rhythm first encountered at the initial beachhead. Remarkably, the sonority imagined is exactly as in the final score, with the rhythm framed by a high chord (subsequently marked *flageoletti*) and uneasy bass line.

These rotations have a continuation in the zigzag line which had been in Stravinsky's mind for some weeks, since the sheets of sketches for *The Nightingale*.[26] It is possible that Stravinsky suddenly noticed the underlying connection between the zigzag and his other ideas, the theme of 'Mystic Circles' for one. Both have an asymmetrical shape, with a 'push' at the end of the phrase. All the signs are that this 'charm' motif (as the zigzag became) was the breakthrough. Stravinsky's first step[27] is to include it as a melodic thread within the texture described above (as at fig. 88), then to arrange it as a duet, here for violas instead of the eventual choice of muted trumpets (fig. 86, see Ex. 5.5).[28] Stravinsky underlines its importance, marking it 'The very beginning of the 2nd tableau'. At once the music which will immediately precede 'Mystic Circles' crystallises, very much as we find it in the final score (figs. 89–91), and with the 'curtain' correctly indicated. Spread over a pair of sheets and dated 11 March, this sketch brings to an end this phase of work on Part II.

The sketches for 'Glorification of the Chosen One'[29] reveal less of Stravinsky's way of working than the earlier sketches for Part II simply because, in this more pianistic music, much is fully formed before it is written down. The working out of the nagging repetitions must have been a trial to anyone within earshot of Stravinsky's piano: 'continued in the next issue' he writes in self mockery.[30]

'Evocation of the Ancestors', the section which follows, seems to have been a spur-of-the-moment inspiration. Unlike any other section of the *Rite*, there are no sketches in advance: the first and only preliminary sketch coming at the very end of work on 'Glorification', entered sideways as an afterthought in the margin. The trigger for this idea seems to have been the rhythm as initially sketched for fig. 115 + 2 in the middle section of 'Glorification'. Once this idea was conceived, Stravinsky seems to have composed 'Evocation' in a single sweep. His one doubt seems to have been the tempo and character of the music, as is shown by the false start which heads the next sheet. Stravinsky has thought of linking 'Glorification' with 'Evocation' by detaching the ♫ ♩ figure and transferring it – thunderously – to the bass. Thus it comes to rest on D♯ (notated E♭ in the sketch); and at first he thinks of the upper harmony in terms of E♭7 chords, a throwback perhaps to the hammered chords of 'Augurs of Spring', whose 'right hand' component is also E♭7. As Craft notes,[31] the syncopations in the bass in this abortive sketch might suggest a maestoso tempo, an initial thought which – it is interesting to note – would linger on in all Stravinsky's recordings of the *Rite*.

Thanks to an earlier sketch[32] the opening of 'Ritual Action of the Ancestors' was already clear in Stravinsky's mind: as a result he goes straight into full score. The gruppetti, formerly on bassoon, are now scored for cor anglais, but still in a 'square' rhythm of even de-misemiquavers which Stravinsky would later nudge off-centre by grouping within a triplet. Sketches for the main body of the movement (figs. 131–9) occupy only four sheets, so that much must therefore be missing. Their interest lies in the evolution in tandem of the two main ideas. One is what Craft calls the 'snake charming' for alto flute, originally imagined two octaves lower, scored for bassoons! Apart from this, there is the evolution of a melody found at the top of a much earlier sheet[33] while Stravinsky was beginning to collect ideas for 'Glorification'. Stravinsky's first variant of this – a frisky melody for solo oboe – makes an unlikely parent to the solemn theme for three trumpets which steals in at fig. 132 and the subsequent apocalyptic outbursts at figs. 134 and 138.

At the end of the sketches for 'Ritual Action' we encounter the most startling difference in the entire work between original conception and final score.[34] Here, amazingly, as the line unravels with the solo for bass clarinet, Stravinsky writes 'End of the Second Part of the *Sacre* (after the "Sacrificial Dance")'. Thus the stuttering septuplet, which we know as the springboard for the 'Sacrificial Dance', is the music to which the Chosen One would have expired – and to make this absolutely clear the sketch concludes with a double bar and a firm 'The End'.

What can this mean? Craft assumes that Stravinsky's note to himself – 'after the Sacrificial Dance' – is to be taken at face value.[35] But is this plausible? The passage marked 'The End' is after all clearly integral to 'Ritual Action' – the presence of the staccato ostinato alone is proof of that. And is it conceivable that Stravinsky could have made this dying fall on the bass clarinet a satisfactory coda to the 'Sacrificial Dance' in anything like the form we know?

Moreover at this point in the sketches nothing exists of the 'Sacrificial Dance' except for a single marginal jotting[36] – in sharp contrast to Stravinsky's practice throughout the rest of the *Rite* of allowing his ideas to run on ahead. What if the 'Sacrificial Dance' had already been composed? The working title 'Action of the Ancestors' could refer only to the opening of the movement (as the Elders assemble to witness the dance), while the 'snake-charming' on alto flute – which it should be noted is an instrument already associated with the maidens (see the solo at fig. 93) – is the Chosen One dancing: her dance is engulfed by the shattering climaxes at figs. 134 and 138 which are also climaxes to the entire work. The music for this movement seems to reflect a deliberate desire to bring together many of the *Rite*'s strands in a summative statement. The possibility must be that what is now known as 'Ritual Action' was originally the 'Sacrificial Dance': this would make sense of a movement which, for all its musical splendour, is dramatically something of an embarrassment, delaying the action when all seems ready for the dénouement. What if Stravinsky then realised that dramatically his first 'Sacrificial Dance' was inadequate, and that a further movement needed to be composed, its music on the lines of the orgiastic irregularities discovered in 'Glorification'?

Not only does this reading of the evidence make sense of the music as it stands, but it explains the otherwise very puzzling letter from Stravinsky to Roerich, dated 19 March 1912 and thus probably written at this very point in the unfolding of the sketches. Stravinsky admits that Part II has turned out to be much shorter than they had envisaged – 'It is regrettable that we planned both tableaux to be equal in length. The first will represent almost three-fourths of the whole...'[37] Even allowing for the fact that Stravinsky had not yet envisaged the first part of the 'Introduction' (the music from fig. 79 to fig. 86 which precedes the duet for two trumpets), this would not account for such a large discrepancy in timing between the two halves – unless one also disregards the final 'Sacrificial Dance' as well.

Finally, the sketches for the Sacrificial Dance show every sign of having been composed at speed. The white heat of Stravinsky's inspiration may well have been ignited by panic, as well it might given their date – November (1912), six months or more after the rest of music was complete, with rehearsals imminent.[38] Why the rush, if not for the reason that Stravinsky realised, late in the day, that his ending was inadequate? And the delay in composing the Sacrificial Dance was surely because Stravinsky had hitherto considered the work finished. Further corroboration comes from the first draft score in which the Sacrificial Dance is absent, and the music for Part II begins with the duet for two trumpets.[39]

To understand how Stravinsky composed the 'Sacrificial Dance' it may be helpful to outline the shape of the section. The 'Sacrificial Dance' falls into five sections – A1 B A2 C A3 – with A2 being an exact reprise of A1 (but transposed down a semitone), while C is the first of the two codas, opening with the tumult of drumming at fig. 174. The page illustrated comes from the final section – A3 – in which Stravinsky has turned the opening music of the 'Sacrificial Dance' into a moto perpetuo. The upper part of page 88 (Ex. 2.4) continues from the previous sheet, showing that Stravinsky has conceived the latter half of this final

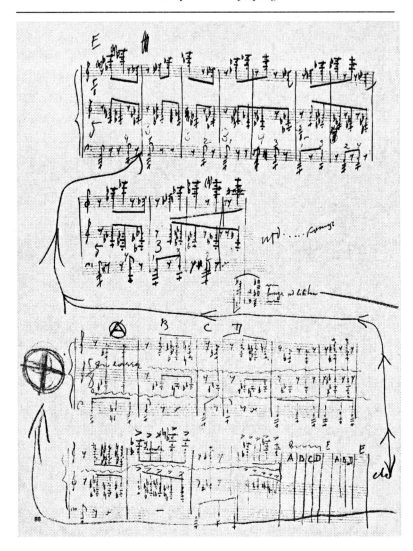

Ex. 2.4 Sacrificial Dance (Sketches, p. 88)

section before its opening. Below we have the preceding passage (as from fig. 186) with all the ideas in place, including the tessitura – as an afterthought Stravinsky has dropped the passage down an octave before raising the stakes in the final bar of the first line (as at fig. 189).

It is now a question of establishing the order and number of repetitions: not for the first time Stravinsky resorts to alphabetical shorthand to indicate how the bars will be shuffled. 'E' refers to the accented interruption (last line second bar), and also (if one follows the arrow looping up the page) the new 'cell' derived from it with which the music now continues (see fig. 192). The arrow also indicates that Stravinsky's initial idea was to interleave the two families of cells – which in the end were kept independent.

'E' is a simple transposition of an idea from the first section (A1). There it is used initially as an interruption before being given the final say (see fig. 148). In the final section Stravinsky links A1 with A3 not only in their ideas but in their structure, by again allowing 'E' first to infiltrate and then to take over.

The first sketch for the opening bars[40] makes clear why, originally, the pause came *before* the first explosive chord – since the bottom D was the end of the previous movement (originally, as we have seen, the end of the work). Stravinsky evidently toyed with the idea of converting the pause into a sustained chord with brass tremolandi and a huge crescendo to *fff*. Another difference from the final version is the notation (in crotchets and quavers) which Stravinsky later diminished (as he explained to Craft)[41] so that rhythmic groupings could be shown by the beams of quavers and semiquavers.

The sketches for the 'Sacrificial Dance' have other examples of Stravinsky's composing shorthand. The A2 section – the reprise of the 'exposition' which was to play a crucial role in Stravinsky's strategy for engineering an explosive finality to the last chord of the *Rite* – appears not at all, being represented simply by a note in bold pencil reminding Stravinsky to go to the start of the timpani rampage (fig. 174) only 'after transposing the whole page [i.e. the exposition] to C♯ major'. A refinement of the alphabetical method is used to plot the repetitions at the climax of the first coda (fig. 184).[42] Here having labelled each bar – A, B, C, D – Stravinsky indicates the continuation with A2, B2 etc., the '2' being the number of (crotchet) beats in the bar.

Stravinsky's first intention – indicated by a note in the margin – was to follow this with a return to the home tonality of D at the start of the final section (fig. 186) . He has the much better idea of continuing with the A in the bass which has underpinned the orgiastic hullabaloo (figs.

Ex. 2.5 Sketches p. 104. Progression from Sacrificial Dance (see fig. 161) copied by Stravinsky before composing the first part of the Introduction to Part II (figs. 79–86)

181–6): as a result the opening of 'Sacrificial Dance' now returns in A rather than in D. Thus was born the idea of this final section being rooted in a dominant pedal which, fuelled by the ever more expanded and unstable versions of cell 'E' (see illustration from the *Sketches*), cries out for resolution – Stravinsky's solution to the problem of creating an ending which would seem final.

Fittingly Stravinsky's last act[43] is to find the exit chord from the climax to the first coda, underlining where it will go with an 'A' in the margin together with a message scribbled below that this will join the music eight sheets earlier, on the lower half of page 88 (Ex. 2.4). Thus the last link is forged – and, scrawled diagonally across the upper half of the page, 'Today, 4/17 November 1912, Sunday, with an unbearable toothache I finished the music of the *Sacre*. I. Stravinsky, Clarens, Châtelard Hotel.'[44]

Again Stravinsky was being premature. Now, for a second time, he must have taken a critical look at Part II, reconsidering the opening which at this stage began with the duet for two trumpets, the 'charm' motif. Was this too flimsy, coming as it would in the wake of the hurricane that ends Part I, 'Dance of the Earth'?

The sketches for a further preliminary section to the 'Introduction' show Stravinsky – for the first time in the composition of the *Rite* – making a conscious architectural decision in advance of developing his ideas. In order to link the beginning of Part II with the end, Stravinsky copies a progression from 'Sacrificial Dance' – the seven chords which climax the 'B' section (at fig. 161). As Ex. 2.5 shows, the chords yield the progression in bar 1, with the push from D minor to the chord of E7 with its octatonic,[45] major–minor colouring – this being the first manifestation of the *idée fixe*, the motivic idea that permeates Part II – together with the modulating sequence which takes the music away from D (see fig. 82). To these Stravinsky adds another layer, again with a view to the introductory character of the music, the high descant which will become the theme of 'Mystic Circles'.

At this point a transition is needed to bridge this with the duet for two trumpets. This was the final problem Stravinsky set himself, and its solution (figs. 84–6) would prove elusive, coming as late as the end of March 1913, with the première only weeks away.

3

Rehearsals and first performance

Stravinsky began work on 2 September 1911. The first unveiling of the score came in November 1911 at the home of Misia Sert in Paris when Stravinsky played what he had so far composed to Diaghilev and others.[1] Stravinsky described the occasion in a letter to Benois: 'I played ... what I had composed of the Sacre ... Everyone liked it very much.'[2]

Part I having been completed on 7 January 1912, Stravinsky recommenced work on 1 March, on the explosive sketch for 'Glorification of the Chosen One'. On 7 March he writes to Andrey Rimsky-Korsakov, 'My God, what happiness it will be for me when I hear it. It seems as if I am indulging in a bit of self-praise. But if you hear it, then you will understand what you and I have to talk about. It is as if twenty and not two years had passed since *The Firebird* was composed.'[3] Strangely (and contradicting the evidence of the sketches) Stravinsky in his letter still seems to believe that the work – which he refers to as *Les Sacres du Printemps* – will be performed in the 1912 *Ballets Russes* season in Paris (which will commence on 10 May).

On 17 March, Stravinsky writes to his mother describing a meeting in Monte Carlo at which he performed the *Rite* to Diaghilev – 'He and Nijinsky were wild about it.' Two days later he writes to Roerich, the first letter since the previous September: '... it seems to me that I have penetrated the secret of the rhythm of Spring, and that musicians will feel it'.[4] By 26 March it is clear that the *Rite* has to be postponed. Stravinsky's letter to Benois with this news also implies that the choreographer was still to be Fokine, who is 'too busy with other ballets, especially Ravel's *Daphnis et Chloë*'.[5]

In April 1912 another of Stravinsky's collaborators heard the *Rite* for the first time. This was the conductor, Pierre Monteux, who recalled – 'With only Diaghilev and myself for an audience, Stravinsky sat down to

26

play a piano reduction of the entire [*sic*] score. Before he got very far I was convinced he was raving mad... The very walls resounded as Stravinsky pounded away, occasionally stamping his feet and jumping up and down...'[6] In another account Monteux ascribes probably the same occasion to summer 1912. 'The room was small and the music was large, the sound of it completely dwarfing the poor piano on which the composer was pounding, completely dwarfing Diaghilev and his poor conductor listening in utter amazement... The old upright piano quivered and shook as Stravinsky tried to give us an idea of his new work... I remember vividly his dynamism and his sort of ruthless impetuosity as he attacked the score. By the time he had reached the second tableau, his face was so completely covered with sweat that I thought, "He will surely burst, or have a syncope." My own head ached badly, and I must admit I did not understand one note of *Le Sacre du Printemps*. My one desire was to flee that room...'[7]

On 9 June came the legendary meeting with Debussy at which the two composers played through Stravinsky's four-hand arrangement. The occasion was described by Louis Laloy: 'One bright afternoon in the spring of 1912 I was walking about my garden with Debussy. We were expecting Stravinsky. As soon as he saw us, the Russian musician ran with his arms outstretched to embrace the French master, who, over his shoulder, gave me an amused but compassionate look. Stravinsky had brought an arrangement for four hands of his work, the *Rite of Spring*. Debussy agreed to play the bass. Stravinsky asked if he could remove his collar. His sight was not improved by his glasses, and, pointing his nose to the keyboard, and sometimes humming a part that had been omitted from the arrangement, he led into a welter of sound the supple, agile hands of his friend. Debussy followed without a hitch and seemed to make light of the difficulty. When they had finished, there was no question of embracing, nor even of compliments. We were dumbfounded, overwhelmed by this hurricane which had come from the depths of the ages, and which had taken life by the roots.'[8] In a subsequent letter (5 November 1912) Debussy wrote – 'I still remember the performance of *Le sacre du printemps* at Laloy's... It haunts me like a good nightmare, and I try in vain to recover the impression. For this reason I await the performance like a gluttonous child to whom sweets have been promised.'[9]

Later that summer there were two further auditions: on 24 August at Lugano (for Diaghilev, Nijinsky and Benois), and around 2 September in Venice to Diaghilev, Nijinsky and Misia Sert – the score was now complete up to fig. 99, the music which immediately precedes the 'tocsins' in 'Mystic Circles'.[10] By November Stravinsky had given a preview to others beyond the immediate Diaghilev circle. Florent Schmitt, who was carefully cultivated as a sympathetic critic by Diaghilev and Stravinsky, wrote ecstatically – 'In a faraway pavilion of Auteuil, which henceforth will remind me of the most magnificent of temples, M. Igor Stravinsky played his *Les Sacres* [*sic*] *du Printemps* for my friends. I will one day tell you of its unforeseen beauty ... the piece tells of freedom, newness and the richness of life.'[11]

Marie Rambert gives a vivid account of Stravinsky at rehearsal – 'When Stravinsky first came to one of our rehearsals and heard the way his music was being played, he blazed up, pushed aside the fat German pianist, nicknamed 'Kolossal' by Diaghilev, and proceeded to play twice as fast as we had been doing and twice as fast as we could possibly dance. He stamped his feet on the floor and banged his fist on the piano and sang and shouted...'[12] On 14 December Stravinsky thanks Roerich enthusiastically for his costume designs – 'they are a real miracle'. At the same time he hints that all is not going well with the rehearsals – 'How I hope that Nijinsky has time enough to stage the 'Spring': it is very complex, and I feel that it must be done as nothing has ever been done before!'[13] Meanwhile Roerich writes that the set designs have been simplified, eliminating superfluous trees – 'a definite improvement'.[14]

Early in the new year (1913) rehearsals had reached a state of crisis. On 2 January Diaghilev telegraphs Stravinsky from Budapest – 'Unless you come here immediately for fifteen days, the Sacre will not take place.'[15] By 25 January Nijinsky had choreographed only the first two dances, up to 'Spring Rounds'. The excuse was the difficulty of creating and rehearsing a new ballet with progress undermined by the punishing schedule of travel and performances. 'I squeezed as much out of these rehearsals as I could, and if I am able to continue this way, I will possibly have enough time for everything – without damaging my health and at the same time dancing well at the performances.'[16]

All winter Monteux[17] had been studying the score daily with Stravinsky at the piano. On 30 March Monteux writes detailing passages in which the orchestration needs modifying. The letter is business-like and laconic.

> From my first telegram you will have understood that, not having rehearsed in the hall of the Theatre [*des Champs-Elysées*], I cannot tell you what *Le Sacre* will produce when the orchestra is in place. Nevertheless, and in comparison with *Firebird* and *Petrushka*, which I have rehearsed in the same hall, the *Sacre* sounds at least as good as your two elder children. The passages to which I refer and which perhaps will need to be slightly altered are the following: At 28, beginning with measure 5, I do not hear the horns loudly enough (unless the rest of the orchestra plays *pp*). And if I make a little *crescendo*, I do not hear them at all. At 37, measures 3 and 4, it is impossible to hear a single note of the flute accompanied by four horns and four trumpets *ff*, and first and second violins, also *ff*. The first flute plays the theme alone in the middle of all this noise. At 41, measures 1 and 2, you have, first the *tubas*, which, in spite of *ff*, produce only a very weak sound; second, the seventh and eighth horns, which one does not hear at all in the low register; third, the trombones, which are extremely loud; fourth, the first six horns, which one hears only moderately in comparison with the trombones. I have added the fourth horn to the seventh and eighth, but without achieving an equilibrium for the four groups. One hears: 1. *mf.* 2. nothing 3. *ff.* 4. *f.* At 65, measure 3, the first four horns have *ff*, but they play with mutes, and I can hear them only with difficulty. This is all that seems to me not to sound the way you want it . . . What a pity that you could not come to these rehearsals, above all for the *Sacre*, and that you did not attend the revelation of your work. I have thought about you a great deal and regretted your absence . . .[18]

An amazing feature of this letter – a symptom perhaps of Monteux's celebrated *sangfroid*, which would stand him in good stead at the first performance – is that there is no mention of the work's difficulties. Equally surprising was that Stravinsky meekly implemented all Monteux's suggestions. There seems indeed to be something fatalistic about Stravinsky in the run-up to the première, as if he had done his best and now washed his hands of the whole enterprise. This might explain the other surprising fact, that he seems deliberately to have avoided the rehearsals, quite unlike his normal practice and in marked contrast to his highly-charged presence at rehearsals for the ballet.[19]

The uproar at the première took the company by surprise. The dress rehearsal had gone perfectly: after months of painstaking rehearsal the dancers had mastered the work's difficulties and even the sceptical Grigoriev, *régisseur* of the *Ballets Russes*, acknowledged the originality and dynamism of Nijinsky's choreography.[20]

At the same time, Diaghilev took the offensive, ensuring support for the new ballet with a generous distribution of free tickets.[21] By a quirk in the design of the new *Théâtre des Champs-Elysées* there was an ambulatory between the boxes of the dress circle, and it was here that Diaghilev's supporters gathered. Thus, as Cocteau described it, the 'smart audience, in tails and tulle, diamonds and ospreys were interspersed with the suits and *bandeaux* of the æsthetic crowd. The latter would applaud novelty simply to show their contempt for the people in the boxes ... Innumerable shades of snobbery, super-snobbery and inverted snobbery were represented ... The audience played the role that was written for it ...'[22]

With detractors and supporters in such proximity, it was inevitable that the first shouts and hisses should in their turn be noisily denounced. Before long the sound of the orchestra was drowned by the commotion and the music, as Marie Rambert remembered, could no longer be heard on stage: the dancers relied instead on Nijinsky, in the wings, shouting out the numbers of their counting schemes.[23] Beside him was his sister, Bronislava, fearful that her brother would add to the scandal by rushing out onto the stage.[24]

Valentine Gross, whose studies of the *Ballets Russes* were exhibited in the foyer, was standing with the supporters. 'The theatre seemed to be shaken by an earthquake. It seemed to shudder. People shouted insults, howled and whistled ... There was slapping and even punching. Words are inadequate to describe such a scene ...'[25] At the end of Part I the police were called , but as soon as the lights dimmed and the music resumed so did the protests, now with a satirical edge: the gestures of the circling maidens, heads tilted on their hands, ridiculed by cries of '*Un docteur, un dentiste, deux dentistes*'.[26] Diaghilev, who had been shouting instructions from his box, moved to the gallery and could be heard imploring for calm, '*Je vous en prie. Laissez s'achever le spectacle.*'[27] For Stravinsky, the hero of the hour was the imperturbable Monteux – 'I was sitting in the fourth or fifth row on the right, and the image of Monteux's back is more vivid in my mind today than the picture of the stage. He stood there apparently impervious and nerveless as a crocodile.'[28] Monteux remembered never once looking at the stage; eyes fixed on the score, he concentrated on rendering 'the exact tempo Igor had given me and which, I must say, I have never forgotten'.[29]

The one consolation was the publicity value of such an evening. The *Rite*, at least, could hardly be ignored, unlike Nijinsky's other première, *Jeux*, which had met with indifference two weeks earlier, on 15 May. Stravinsky later recalled the mixture of emotions: 'We were excited, angry, disgusted, and ... happy ... Diaghilev's only comment was: "Exactly what I wanted." He certainly looked contented... Quite probably he had already thought about the possibility of such a scandal when I first played him the score, months before, in the east corner ground room of the Grand Hotel in Venice.'[30]

Part II

The music

4

Language

Melody

Before the 1960s the best description of the melodies in the *Rite* would have been that they are 'folk like'. Only one – the bassoon solo that opens the work – was acknowledged by Stravinsky to be a folk tune. So he told his biographer André Schæffner in 1931, later reinforcing the point – 'The opening bassoon in *Le Sacre du Printemps* is the only folk melody in that work.'[1]

Among the first to see the newly emerged sketches (in the late 1960s) was Robert Craft, who noted that a number of entries seemed to have been copied down, and surmised that these were probably from folk sources. Craft seems not to have had the idea of checking these against the Juskiewicz anthology – a collection of 1,785 Lithuanian folk songs – which had been mentioned by Schæffner. It was not until the late 1970s that they were tracked to their source by Lawrence Morton.[2]

The five tunes identified by Morton as deriving from the anthology all occur early in the *Rite*. Taruskin has shown that they were especially appropriate to the *Rite*, being 'songs associated with the very festivals on which Roerich based the scenario'.[3] It may well be that it was Roerich who alerted Stravinsky to the Juskiewicz collection. Yet if Stravinsky's aim was authenticity, his selection from Juskiewicz was extraordinarily perfunctory. Three of the tunes are taken from entries which occur at the lower right corner of their pages, as if with the book in one hand and pen in the other Stravinsky chose tunes on the basis of a 'cursory riffling of the pages'.[4] Moreover since the Juskiewicz borrowings occur only early on (in the 'Introduction', 'Augurs of Spring' and 'Spring Rounds') it seems that Stravinsky did not bother to take the book with him when he moved to Switzerland in late September, 1911.

35

Ex. 4.1a

Juskiewicz no.157

Introduction

Lento ♩ = 50 tempo rubato

Ex. 4.1b

Juskiewicz no.34

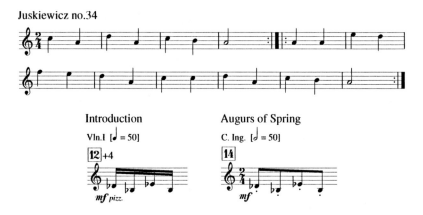

The five melodies, in the order in which Stravinsky's adaptations of them appear in the *Rite*, are shown in Ex. 4.1. Two of Stravinsky's versions – Exx. 4.1a and d – preserve the shape and for the most part intervals of the original, although in Ex. 4.1e (which conflates two tunes) the opening of the first source tune is adapted, presumably in order to fit the pentatonic shape of the second. The rhythmic freedoms, together

Ex. 4.1c

Juskiewicz no.787

Augurs of Spring

[Tempo giusto ♩ = 50]

Ex. 4.1d

Juskiewicz no.142

Ritual of Abduction

Presto ♩· = 132

with the grace notes, are perhaps a restoration of folk style lacking in Juskiewicz's staid transcription. Ex. 4.1d (from 'Ritual of Abduction') is also pretty faithful, the most notable change being Stravinsky's decision to flatten the leading note from D to D♭ – in the sketches Stravinsky copied the tune in E♭ minor (with G naturals), the original being in E♭ major.

The other two versions (Exx. 4.1b and c) are so rudimentary that it could well be that Stravinsky arrived at a similar result independently. In the end the combination of the narrow range of intervals in the folk models, in conjunction with Stravinsky's streamlining methods, make it

Ex. 4.1e

Juskiewicz no.249

Juskiewicz no.271

Spring Rounds

Tranquillo ♩ = 108

difficult to disentangle what is his and what is borrowed: there may well be many more folk tunes in the *Rite* which will never be recognised, not only because we do not know their source, but also because Stravinsky changed his borrowed melodies beyond recognition.

These difficulties are highlighted in Ex. 4.2. Ex. 4.2a is a tune copied by Stravinsky not from Juskiewicz but from a collection of folksong arrangements by Rimsky.[5] Both van den Toorn and Taruskin see this as the source for the answering phrase in 'Spring Rounds' and the ensuing vivo. At first glance the link seems tenuous. If the melody really was used it shows just how much Stravinsky was prepared to distort his models in order to conform with the *Rite*'s repertoire of melodic types.

Indeed the way Stravinsky adapted his sources seems to have been designed to create a web of inter-related melodies. Ex. 4.3 shows all the principal melodies of the *Rite*. One could imagine this as a family tree with two main stems. One is formed by step-wise melodies using the intervals tone–semitone–tone within the compass of a perfect fourth,

Ex. 4.2a Sketches, p. 8

Ex. 4.2b Sketches, p. 8 (Spring Rounds after fig. 49)

Ex. 4.2c Spring Rounds

the so-called 'minor tetrachord'; in the other the intervals of fourths and seconds predominate. Naturally there are overlaps between the two stems. A simple example is the ostinato from 'Augurs of Spring' – Db–Bb–Eb–Bb. Another, more extended, is the transition before 'Spring Rounds' – Eb–C–Eb–C–Bb etc. (see Ex. 4.3n).[6]

The family tree is most apparent in the 'Introduction', the section of the *Rite* richest and most varied in its melodies, which come together in the swarming tutti at fig. 10. In the wake of this chattering tumult, the return of the opening bassoon solo a regretful semitone lower seems like an *envoi* to the 'Introduction's' garden of melody, before the real business of the ballet gets underway.

Harmony

The dissonance of the 'Augurs' chord is naked, brutal and repeated with an insistence unprecedented in art-music before the *Rite*. Such dissonance so mesmerised early critics that for a long time the *Rite*'s harmony was regarded as arbitrary. Even Edward J. Dent – who was broadly

Ex. 4.3a Introduction

Lento ♩ = 50 tempo rubato

Ex. 4.3b Introduction

Ex. 4.3c Introduction

Ex. 4.3d Introduction

Ex. 4.3e Introduction

Ex. 4.3f Introduction

Ex. 4.3g Augurs of Spring

Ex. 4.3h Augurs of Spring

Ex. 4.3i Augurs of Spring

Ex. 4.3j Augurs of Spring

Ex. 4.3k Augurs of Spring

Ex. 4.3l Ritual of Abduction

Presto ♩. = 132

Ex. 4.3m Ritual of Abduction

Ex. 4.3n Spring Rounds

Tranquillo ♩ = 108

Ex. 4.3o

Ritual of Abduction

Ritual of the Rival Tribes

Molto allegro ♩ = 168

Ex. 4.3p Ritual of the Rival Tribes

Ex. 4.3q Dance of the Earth

Ex. 4.3r Mystic Circles of the Young Girls

Ex. 4.3s Mystic Circles of the Young Girls

Ex. 4.3t Ritual Action of the Ancestors

Ex. 4.3u Ritual Action of the Ancestors

Ex. 4.4 Motto chord from Augurs

sympathetic – described the sound of the *Rite* as noise. For Dent the
Rite negated the idea of music as a language – '... what is baffling is a
form of speech which entirely ignores those principles of syntax which
we have been brought up to regard as logical and inevitable ...
[Stravinsky] does not pretend to argue; he just makes noises at us. Some
think them horrible, some find them fascinating...'[7]

The 'Augurs' chord seems the right place to begin a search for any
logic there may be in the harmony of the *Rite*: not only was it
Stravinsky's point of departure, but its presence – vast, granitic, immo–
bile – has caused writers to refer to it variously as the motto- or ur-chord
(Ex. 4.4). The harmony is in fact made up of tonal chords in dissonant
conjunction. Many of the other dissonances in the *Rite* are formed

Ex. 4.5a Sacrificial Dance

Ex. 4.5b Sacrificial Dance (Sketches, p. 85)

similarly: either from a triad (or dominant seventh) plus a dissonant note, or (as here) from the superimposition of a dominant seventh and a triad. Triads may also be arranged successively, as they are in the woodwind layer in the 'Introduction' to Part II, or as at fig. 144. In this example the succession of chords is clear in its logic, being in fact a sequence, though not a diatonic one. If one were to rearrange the five chords in root position, the root of each chord would track the notes of a diminished seventh arpeggio – a tell-tale sign (Ex. 4.5a) that the music's basis may be the 'octatonic' scale.

Nineteenth-century music, and Russian music in particular, contains isolated and usually fortuitous examples of octatonic writing. However, Stravinsky's teacher, Rimsky-Korsakov, was fascinated to the point of obsession (as his notebooks reveal) by the octatonic scale and its possibilities. In Rimsky's stage works octatonic writing has a symbolic function, being associated with the magical or fantastic, as distinct from the human world which is characterised by diatonic, folk-derived music. This was a device which Stravinsky followed in *Firebird*. The most famous instance in early Stravinsky is 'the' *Petrushka* chord, with its joining of triads a tritone apart (on C and F♯) which, despite the furiously bitonal effect, belong to the same octatonic collection.[8]

The octatonic scale consists of eight steps of alternating semitones and tones. There is a simple way to generate this at the piano. Play with the left hand a diminished seventh – say, C–E♭–F♯–A – and overlap this with the right hand playing a diminished seventh a semitone higher (D♭–E–G–B♭). Then play the notes of each arpeggio alternating

Ex. 4.6

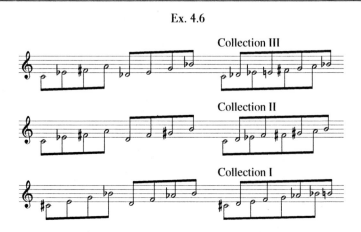

between the hands, and the result will be an octatonic scale. Just as the diminished seventh can only be transposed so that it produces different notes twice, there are only three possible octatonic scales (called 'collections'). It will be noticed also that the left hand arpeggio generates four major and four minor triads together with four dominant sevenths[9] (see Ex. 4.6).

In terms of harmony, then, the characteristic octatonic sound is formed by combining triads either a tritone apart (as in the *Petrushka* chord) or a minor third apart. In 'Augurs' we see this clearly in the first contrasting block, at fig. 14, where the descending cello arpeggio is C major against the continuing Eb7 of the ostinato (Ex. 4.7). This conjunction – C/Eb – continues to be important throughout Part I. We find it, for example, at the opening of 'Ritual of Abduction' (Ex. 4.8), and it runs throughout 'Dance of the Earth', being apparent in the final harmony, left hanging in mid-air by the appallingly abrupt ending.

Stravinsky's use of the octatonic scale in the *Rite* has been exhaustively explored by van den Toorn. His great insight was to see how this thoroughly modern system of harmony was combined by Stravinsky with the melodic characteristics of age-old folk music. To see how this was done one can generate an octatonic scale at the piano by melodic means. First play with the left hand a 'minor tetrachord', that is the lowest four notes of a minor scale – say, G# A# B C#. Now add a similar

Ex. 4.7 Augurs of Spring

Ex. 4.8 Ritual of Abduction

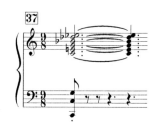

Ex. 4.9

Ex. 4.10 Ritual of the Rival Tribes

tetrachord with the right hand a tritone higher (D E F G): the result is
another octatonic collection (Ex. 4.9). The point is that the 'minor
tetrachord' consists of the intervals (tone–semitone–tone) which as we
have already seen are the basis for the great majority of the *Rite*'s
melodies.

Ex. 4.11a Ritual of the Rival Tribes

etc.

Ex. 4.11b

Ex. 4.10 shows this theory in practice. The excerpt comes from the border between 'Ritual of the Rival Tribes' and the 'Procession of the Sage' where two melodies mingle and clash (fig. 64). Both are tetrachords (though in the lower one the B is missing), set a tritone apart and thus octatonic. From this point of view, the F♯ is regarded by van den Toorn as 'ornamental'.[10] There are, however, a number of objections. In the lower (tuba) line, Stravinsky alternates F♯ with G♮. What if one hears (as I do) the G♮, rather than the F♯, as 'ornamental'? This would be a perfectly plausible 'reading', since the F♯ is consistently used as the upbeat to the bar of crotchets, G♯ A♯ C♯ A♯, there being only one exception. A further complication is that the tune in the upper line is thickened in thirds (Ex. 4.11a). In octatonic terms this gives yet another foreign note; the C. But to describe C as foreign is absurd, since these treble thirds are clearly based around a C major triad. In other words, the octatonic explanation misses the musical point.

In favour of the octatonic reading is the fact that in the sketches the B♭ is notated as A♯.[11] The point is emphasised by Taruskin: 'The spelling betokens Stravinsky's fastidious recognition of the pitch in question as belonging to the 'other' tetrachord, and shows how fundamental the octatonic bias was to his conceptualisation of the passage in the act of composing it.'[12] By 'other' tetrachord, Taruskin means C♯ B A♯ G♯, the pitches which complement G F E D in the octatonic scale. Van den Toorn's answer is an ingenious refinement to octatonic theory. He proposes that in the *Rite* the upper tetrachord (G F E D) may combine either with one a tritone lower – making the octatonic scale – or on occasion with one a fifth lower, making a Dorian scale: G F E D C B♭ A G (see Ex. 4.11b).

What is clear is that throughout the *Rite* octatonic collections are combined with other elements – diatonic, modal or frankly dissonant. No doubt, as a former pupil of Rimsky-Korsakov, Stravinsky's ear was guided instinctively towards the octatonic scale and the harmonies derived from it. Nonetheless, the sketches for the *Rite* provide the evidence that Stravinsky was not working with systematic reference to octatonic collections. This is absolutely clear when one studies those chords which, between the first sketch and final score, gradually evolve towards octatonic forms. Taruskin cites, for example, the seven chords that climax the second section of the 'Sacrificial Dance'. These went through three different versions before Stravinsky was satisfied, on the way becoming octatonically more regular.[13] A less complicated but equally telling instance comes in the sketches for the 'Sacrificial Dance' (see Exx. 4.5a and 4.5b). Here the crucial change is made on the spur of the moment in a tangle of crossings-out, while Stravinsky was in the process of making the continuity sketch.[14] Apparently spontaneously, the descending sequence of five chords is altered to create a pure octatonic progression. Had Stravinsky been referring to the octatonic scale while composing, his chords would undoubtedly have been octatonic from the outset.

In 'Ritual of Abduction' the masses of harmony (together with the explosions in the bass) are octatonic, but are overlaid by a melody centred on an alien D major triad (van den Toorn prefers to describe this as based on a Dorian scale, from A to A).[15] In 'Dance of the Earth' three elements combine. The ostinato, which is in whole tones, shares pitches with the octatonic melody lines, while the chordal punctuations are largely diatonic (C major). In other words, Stravinsky uses octatonic writing as part of an eclectic mix, with the same undogmatic freedom with which he adapted borrowed folk melodies. In some respects the weakest passages in the *Rite* are those which are most purely octatonic: lacking 'grit', they run on the spot. See 'Ritual of Abduction', figs. 42–3, for example.

What all the foregoing examples have in common is *dissonance*. In 'Rival Tribes' the conflict between upper and lower melodies at fig. 64 is accentuated by the constant jarring of G/G♯ on the first of each bar. In 'Augurs' this same dissonance – the 'diminished octave' – is set between the upper and lowest notes: E♭/E. Taruskin, taking these as his basis,

Ex. 4.12 Interlocking 'fourths' chords at the 11/4 bar before Glorification

proposes a *Grundgestalt* formed by adding the lower note (B♭) of the
E♭–B♭ tetrachord. The resulting three-note chord – E♭ B♭ E – may be
inverted within the same outer pitches (E♭ A E).[16]

This 'fourths' chord – so called because made up of two fourths, one
perfect, the other augmented – is heard in the famous 11/4 bar which
unleashes 'Glorification', a movement permeated throughout with the
sound of this chord (Ex. 4.12). Elsewhere the chord has a major–minor
effect. This is clear in Part II in the section which develops the duet for
two trumpets. Here E♭ B♭ E are rooted in C, and the harmonies oscillate
between this sound and a parallel harmony rooted on B♭. Elsewhere,
though not arising from the *Grundgestalt*, major–minor clashes are
frequent. One occurs in the opening bassoon solo, where the bassoon's
C♮ is heard in a false relation with C♯ on the horn (Ex. 4.3a). Other
instances include that in 'Mystic Circles', where Stravinsky combines
triads of B major and B minor (Ex. 5.6), and in the clashing major and
minor thirds which open 'Rival Tribes'. The richest example of the
sound comes in the 'Introduction' to Part II, in the second bar (fig.
79 + 2), where the dissonance is between G♯ (the major third of a
dominant seventh on E) and the high G♮ (Ex. 5.3). The same harmony,
massively emphasised, will be part of the climax to the second section of
the 'Sacrificial Dance' (Ex. 5.10).

Having considered the basic 'fourths' chord on its own, we can now
follow examples where a third is added to the upper two notes to make a
triad, as in the harmonies of 'Spring Rounds' (Ex. 4.13). Another is to
make them into a dominant seventh. Notice that the dominant seventh
is always in the first inversion, this being the most compact, punchiest
version, but also the one that ensures that the dissonance with the
diminished octave is exposed in the outer two pitches. Finally, as in
'Augurs', the bass note (E) may also be thickened, to make a polychord
(here E♭7 against E major).

Here is the final significance of the ur- or motto-chord, the fact that

Ex. 4.13 Spring Rounds

Ex. 4.14

Stravinsky chooses to echo it almost exactly in the first harmony of the 'Sacrificial Dance' (Ex. 4.14). This symmetry between the opening dance of Part I and the final dance of Part II is striking, and leads me to consider the degree to which the *Rite* is structured in a tonal plan, something flatly denied by most writers.[17]

As we have seen, Part II is framed by a D tonality. There are strong tonal and thematic links between its 'Introduction' and the 'Sacrificial Dance', and D minor's dominant (A) is used as the basis of the central movement ('Glorification') and as the 'dominant pedal' which acts as the finale to the whole ballet. In Part I the prevailing 'tonality' is E♭,[18] so that the conjunction of chords of D and E♭ in the opening harmony of the 'Sacrificial Dance' seems particularly apt. And it is not for the first time. The main tonal ingredient of 'Ritual of Abduction' is the antipathy between E♭ and D: as this section proceeds, however, the tune in D is 'resolved' to E♭, thus preparing the trills on E♭ which accompany the transition between 'Ritual of Abduction' and the firmly E♭-centred 'Spring Rounds', with its key signature of E♭ minor. At the end of Part I, 'Dance of the Earth' opens with C major in blazing opposition to E major, in the 'fanfares' which derive from the whole-tone thirds of the source melody. But with the arrival of the entry on violas (fig. 75) which ignites the concluding 'prairie-fire'[19] E gives way to E♭. Thus the end of Part I has the same harmonies – E, E♭, C – which we found rotated at the beginning of 'Augurs' (fig. 14). Finally, given that each Part has such

a clear sense of tonal centre – E♭ in Part I, D in Part II – the combining
of the two in the opening chord of the 'Sacrificial Dance' is surely no
accident.

Rhythm

The most famous rhythmic innovation in the *Rite* is found in passages
where metre is in perpetual flux, of which the 'Sacrificial Dance' is the
principal example. This metric disorder forms one of two rhythmic
categories, its counterpart at the other end of the spectrum being
sections where the pulse is rigidly unvarying. This second type reaches
its apogee in the stillness of the penultimate movement, 'Ritual Action
of the Ancestors', the longest and most mesmerising of the *Rite*'s slow
movements.

Where pulse and metre are stable this encourages other types of
disorder. We find this at the very opening of 'Augurs of Spring', where
by the third bar the quavers are already attacked by accents, punched
out by strings and horns. Later, as 'Augurs of Spring' reaches its closing
stages (fig. 28 + 5), the regular surface of the music is disturbed by a
different kind of complication. The music stacks into layers, so that
though the quavers remain constant they form into three different
metres. In the centre of the texture is the ticking ostinato (D♭ B♭ E♭ B♭)
which has been a persistent thread running through the music. This is in
2/4. Meanwhile the cellos and basses, pizzicato, are in 3/4, having an
ostinato which repeats its pattern every three crotchet beats, while the
premonition of 'Spring Rounds' (the tune on the trumpets) is a march-
like 4/4. This accumulation of layers is a forerunner of the huge metrical
and sonic meltdown in 'Procession of the Sage', another 'march', which
brings Part I to a crisis.

Where the barring is irregular there may be a number of explanations.
At its simplest the time signatures may change because they follow the
natural stress of the melody – a sign of the *Rite*'s origins in Slavic folk
music where such irregularities are a characteristic. An example is the
tune from 'Mystic Circles', which if not a folk tune (and it may be) is
certainly very like one (Ex. 4.3r).

Typically the undulations of the 'Mystic Circles' melody are forced
to compete with an ostinato (cello pizzicato) which can scarcely be

termed an 'accompaniment' since it occupies its own rigidly independent metre (2/4). This is another unprecedented feature of the *Rite*, the way Stravinsky combines line with line, layer with layer, in such a way that they retain a reptilian indifference to one another. This is one source of the lack of sentiment or 'pity' for which the *Rite* was famous and which still has its power to disturb. The lack of expressive 'contact' between ideas is found also in the total lack of reaction as one event follows another. The most spectacular results of this occur at the great escarpments, where a welter of competing lines abruptly sheers off in a way that leaves the edges as jagged as possible.

For these reasons the *Rite* is often described in terms of more or less independent 'blocks'. But how true is this? At the opening of 'Augurs of Spring' (fig. 13) one might regard these chords as 'pure' rhythm, since melody and harmonic movement are in suspension. Thus the rhythm is simply a succession of quavers with irregularly spaced accents. Turn back a page, however, and one finds a transition which provides a very carefully prepared context, one which determines how the quavers will be heard. True, the actual edge between the transition and the 'Augurs' chords is absolutely abrupt; but the crucial connection between the music before and after fig. 13 is unmistakable. The violins (pizzicato) outline the ostinato figure – D♭ B♭ E♭ B♭ – and thus establish a pulse (crotchets) and metre (2/4): the pizzicato semiquavers here (crotchet = 50) equal the quavers at fig. 13 (minim = 50). Hence we hear the accented chords not as a random succession of accents, but as clearly on or off the beat. Furthermore we hear the accents within the shape of the 2/4 metre so that each bar is felt to be either stable or disruptive.

Continue into 'Augurs of Spring' and the music proceeds by switching from block to block, driven always by the motoric quaver rhythm. The first two blocks are juxtaposed antiphonally, the first eight bars scored for strings plus horns, opposite its counterpart, the ostinato on clucking woodwind with a counterpoint of pizzicato cellos. Dramatically and musically this technique has its origins in the first scene of *Petrushka*, in which Stravinsky describes the swirl of the Shrovetide Fair in a collage of brilliantly characterised vignettes which he then 'cuts' together like a film editor; each block belongs to a stream of music, woven together with other streams just as a director intercuts different angles of view of a scene, or as a 'cubist' artist incorporates disparate

elements within a picture or sculpture to capture more of its 'reality'
than can be seen from a single viewpoint.[20]
    Although the sharp edges between one block and another keep them
separate, the blocks are interdependent in all sorts of ways. One can see
this by tracking the subtle shifts in rhythmic emphasis as 'Augurs'
proceeds. At the outset, as we have seen, we hear the quavers in a clear
framework of pulse and metre. Nonetheless the ferocity and unex-
pectedness of each accent may make us begin to lose our bearings. If so,
order is firmly restored at the next block (fig. 14) which takes up the
violins' pizzicato ostinato again, now on cor anglais. At the same time as
restoring the pulse and metre, this block effects a subtle change. At fig.
14 the lowest line – pizzicato cellos – changes harmony only once per bar
and follows a rising and falling shape which clearly outlines a minim
pulse. Stravinsky measured the tempo of 'Augurs' in minims ($\downarrow$ = 50),
with the pattern repeating every two bars. Thus when the hammered
chords resume (fig. 14 + 5) we tend to hear the bars in pairs. As a result
the game between pulse and syncopation undergoes a sort of rhythmic
modulation so that now we hear it as a contest between bars – between
those which are 'stable' and those which contain one or more syncopations. In the end the opposition between the two has a thematic outcome
(fig. 19) in the tune of the 'old woman' (Exx. 4.3i and 2.3b). It is clear,
then, that Stravinsky's rhythmic mastery is not a matter of just the
rhythms he invents, but of the way he engineers a context in which they
are heard correctly and hence to the maximum effect. Furthermore
these rhythms are not static, but because of their changing context are in
a perpetual state of evolution.
    We have seen (in the transition before fig. 13) how Stravinsky
establishes a regular pulse and metre. The move the opposite way is
illustrated marvellously by the *Rite*'s most important transition, which
comes before the 'Sacrificial Dance' (before fig. 142). Here Stravinsky's
purpose is to break down the implacable quaver rhythm of 'Ritual
Action of the Ancestors' which, as discussed earlier, is the climax of the
unvarying rhythmic type. This he does by interpolating increasingly
ominous silences, and through the improvisatory arabesques of the two
bass clarinets. Yet the trick, worked again with hairbreadth precision, is
to retain just enough sense of the quaver pulse for the ambush to work as
it should. For the first chord of the 'Sacrificial Dance', if it is to be truly

electrifying, *must* be heard as a syncopation[21] – both for the drama of the moment (how pedestrian it sounds as a downbeat) but also so that we make sense of the bass/treble, left hand/right hand pattern which follows.

In 'Augurs' the juggling of bars or pairs of bars, with or without syncopations, is a sign of the 'cell' technique which will reach its height in the 'Sacrificial Dance'. Just as the borrowed folk melodies are stream-lined, the drive to dissect, to pare everything to the essentials, infects the *Rite* at every level. The opening bassoon solo, if properly articulated according to Stravinsky's phrase marks, is not one phrase but five discrete cells. In the first, second and fifth of these the melody circles through the same eight notes, each time with altered rhythm; in this way it conforms to the Stravinsky trademark whereby melodies are varied by realigning them with the natural stress of beat or metre. Meanwhile the third and fourth cells are shorter interpolations, though each ends (as do the other cells) on the tonic, A. Taken together, the five make a shape with a clear profile, complete with tiny 'development' (the third and fourth cells) ending with a taut, compressed restatement.

As melodies divide into cells, so these may reform to create new melodic shapes. The alto flute melody (fig. 93 + 5) is a case in point, its *tesseræ* (Morton's word) making a maze full of unexpected twists and turns so that even those who know the *Rite* well find this melody difficult to recall accurately. Towards the end of 'Mystic Circles' the harmony, too, becomes formulaic, each accompanying chord being 'fixed' with its melody note.[22] In this passage all sense of harmonic movement or function is lost, the chords simply drifting like so many disconnected dabs of colour.

The *Rite*'s great passages of metrical disturbance occur in Part II. There is a forerunner in Part I, however, in the really wild patch of rhythm which climaxes 'Ritual of Abduction' (fig. 46). Here the changes of time signature result from Stravinsky's desire to strike the maximum sparks from the collision between the treble tune and the bass per-cussions which previously, at the movement's opening, have been heard antiphonally. The rhythmic stresses of the tune have been established earlier (fig. 40). Ex. 4.15 gives my reconstruction of the rhythm of fig. 46 as it might have been had Stravinsky preserved the original shape and stress of the tune at the climax. The arrows in this example mark the

Ex. 4.15 Ritual of Abduction
Arrows indicate quaver values omitted by Stravinsky

quavers which are excised in Stravinsky. The effect of Stravinsky's ruthless compression is to make each timpani 'downbeat' so unexpected that it hits home as a sickening jolt. Where my version is feebly predictable, with Stravinsky treble and bass are forced apart into separate rhythmic orbits and thus into ferocious confrontation.

In 'Glorification of the Chosen One', the central scherzo of Part II, the two rhythmic types – stable–unstable – join battle in a thrilling *tour de force*. Before being released the music's energy is coiled like a spring, in the bar of 11/4 crotchets, as massive and monolithic in its repeated down bows as the chords which open 'Augurs of Spring'. Its purpose – as with the pizzicati which earlier gave 'Augurs' its context – is to drum a pulse into our minds. Once underway 'Glorification' juggles three elements. The duple-time 'vamp' is a reminder of the similar trivia which, in *Petrushka*, Stravinsky had already turned to gold. Although in itself crudely regular, the number of the vamp's repetitions, anything but predictable, is designed to keep us guessing: one knows an ambush is coming, but never exactly when. At the other extreme is the chaotic energy of the uprushing scales. Mediating between the two is the movement's main idea, massive and disciplined, yet unstable in its metre (5/8) and stress (Ex. 4.16).

Where indeed – in this 5/8 bar – is the beat? One answer might be the

Ex. 4.16 Glorification of the Chosen One

Ex. 4.17 Sacrificial Dance

Ex. 4.18 Cell X (Sacrificial Dance)

quaver, the lowest common denominator which binds bars of different length; yet these quavers are too quick to form a perceivable pulse. The answer – and this is Stravinsky's great rhythmic innovation in the *Rite* – is that the pulse itself is flexible, commuting here between a crotchet and a dotted crotchet. Even this is ambiguous: do we hear the 5/8 bars as 2 + 3, or 3 + 2? Likewise when these expand to 7/8, do we hear 2 + 2 + 3, or 2 + 3 + 2? Again, the music keeps us guessing.

Stravinsky's manipulation of rhythmic cells is at its most intense in the closing pages of the 'Sacrificial Dance' (from fig. 186). At first glance the impression given by the score is complex, with a succession of bars varying in length (apparently randomly) between units of 5, 4, and 2 semiquavers. Once one understands that the bars operate in pairs – and

Ex. 4.19 Sacrificial Dance

with the second bar of each pair invariant – then the pattern revealed is simple. Ex. 4.17 shows the first four bars at fig. 186. If we label the first bar or 'cell' A5 – where the 5 refers to the number of semiquavers in the bar – and its counterpart (the 2/8 bar) as B, the sequence is as follows:

A5–B, A2–B, A5–B, A5–B, A2–B, A5–(B missing)

The omission of 'B' at this point is a hiccup which triggers the next phase (at fig. 189). The pairing of 'A' and 'B' is reasserted, but now twice interrupted by a third cell, 'X' (Ex. 4.18) – like 'A' and 'B' this too derives from the music of the opening section of 'Sacrificial Dance'.

(fig. 189) A5–B, Interruption, A5, (B omitted), Interruption

then

(figs. 190–2) A5–B, A5–B, A5–B, A2–B

The regularity is clearly intended to clinch the section to this point. Notice that once again it is by breaking the pattern that Stravinsky triggers the next phase.

From fig. 192 two new cells are used, though the first of these (Ex. 4.19) is clearly derived from the 'interruption' (Ex. 4.18). However, unlike the previous phase from fig. 186 to fig. 192, these cells are used only fitfully in tandem as a pair. Eventually, at fig. 195, the second cell drops out of the race altogether. From this point it seems clear that the first cell is itself made up of two segments, the first mobile, the second (consisting of the last two semiquavers) invariant. A glance at the score from fig. 195 onwards shows the inexorable expansion of the 'mobile' element, checked only once at fig. 198, where the cell in its original form

Ex. 4.20 Sacrificial Dance

is restated. After this (fig. 198 + 3) the vertical ties which join the music's left and right hands (so to speak) dissolve. The effect of the bass is to move in even quavers, a semiquaver 'out' with the upper line which likewise could be heard as regular, with a consistent quaver pulse (Ex. 4.20). The *Rite*'s last great rhythmic coup is to force bass and treble back into alignment with the climactic downbeat whack at fig. 201, itself the trigger for another kind of climax, the furthest expansion of the cell.

In this way a sort of double ambiguity arises: the 'foreground' is the rhythm as written, the background a sort of hidden regularity, which, however, by dissolving the relationship between bass and treble (left and right hands) turns this vertically conceived music into two 'horizontal' and independent layers. Thus the final crisis in the *Rite* belies its 'vertical' appearance on the page, having much more in common with the independent rotating layers which make up previous impasses than might at first appear.

5

Commentary

Part I: *Introduction* to *Spring Rounds*

In later life Stravinsky described the music of the 'Introduction' as 'the awakening of nature, the scratching, gnawing, wiggling of birds and beasts'. Yet it is clear from the correspondence with Roerich that at the time he was imagining not a dawn chorus but a human music, the orchestral wind soloists being the piping of *dudki*. The music they play may resemble the cries of birds and animals but its real purpose is to recapture, in imagination at least, a lost musical world. Stravinsky's idea was nothing less than to evoke this, using as his models the sounds of nature, the cries of animals and birds, inflected by the intervals of folk music, the most ancient form of music available to him. The scoring of the opening for bassoon, in an unnaturally high register, has this folk-like timbre: thin and reedy, and, even in expert hands, riskily fragile, a solitary thread of sound drawn from the heart of the huge silent orchestra.

The story of the rest of the 'Introduction' is of how this complete, closed, self-contained statement is prised apart, the music then re-forming fragment by fragment into a series of strands, all of which will come together in the climactic mêlée (figs. 10–12), the first of the *Rite*'s outbursts of disciplined anarchy. The germinal idea which will unravel the opening melody is contained in the three notes on the horn. The first step is for the C♯ to acquire a partner a fourth lower, in a weird reharmonisation of the high C to which the bassoon has returned as if making to restart. Moving in parallel, the fourth, on a clarinet and bass clarinet, slithers unsteadily (poco accelerando) down a complete chromatic scale, thus opening up a chromatic dimension completely foreign to the 'white note' modal A minor of the bassoon melody. The fourths then remind us of their origin in a gentle ricochet, reinforcing the bassoon melody (which has resumed) just as the horn did in the first phrase (bars 2–3). Typically this flashback also looks forward, triggering a series of regular undulations as the chromatic line starts to take shape. Thus the opening three notes on the horn, initially a complement to the bassoon line, have opened an entirely new line of thought.

In this way the *Rite* actually begins with a transition, the first of many, in which new ideas form as old ones decline. In this case the material in decline is the bassoon melody. It is heard twice more, each time shortened, but – significantly – each time in a way that makes it noticeably more purposeful, as its dawdling rhapsodic style is progressively tightened. The effect is to transform the bassoon solo from a tune to a motif, and so bring it within the melodic style of the rest of the 'Introduction'.

Already it is apparent that one aspect of Stravinsky's strategy is to keep ideas as distinct as possible, both horizontally – each separated into its own layer by differences of timbre and rhythm – and by the abruptness with which events follow one another. On the surface, therefore, the music appears as self-contained 'blocks', each defined by motifs which rotate and turn in on themselves, and by the characteristically hard edges between one block and the next.

But the appearance is deceptive. The lines spin out from one another in a web of inter-related melody. It is true that because of the blocks, the pattern of growth is not smooth but happens through sudden spurts. Yet these decisive moments are always carefully engineered, or 'seeded'. Take for example the music at fig. 4 (Ex. 4.3c). The preceding six bars are an interlude which flows out of the final version of the bassoon melody. The music marks time with somewhat directionless elaborations by the cor anglais against the undulating chromatic strand (the parallel fourths). As always in the *Rite*, stillness is a sign that something momentous is about to happen. So it is at fig. 4: at last a settled harmony is formed (E major, second inversion) from which spring entries on the oboe and D clarinet. The timbre of the clarinet cuts through the still somnolent atmosphere, but notice that its line is not new: it picks up from a melodic tentacle trailed by the end of the first bassoon solo (bars 4–5) and heard again (fig. 3 + 2) as an afterthought to the third and last bassoon solo. Now we hear it reasserted decisively, beginning on A♯. In terms of harmony, the D clarinet's A♯, pulled down to E by way of G♮, brings the first 'octatonic' sound of the work when heard in conjunction with the E major triad – against which the oboe's D♯ is persistently foreign.[1] This harmony, too, is beautifully prepared: the shiver of electricity given by the major triad comes after repeated reiterations of E *minor*, which we have heard no fewer than six times outlined in the various versions of the bassoon melody.

But fig. 4 looks forward as well as back. The second inversion triad, once established, will become a central feature. Also important is a persistent rhythmic motif developed by the clarinet at fig. 4 (but heard already, as early as bar 6), a kink in the triplet rhythm caused by the placing of grace notes so that triplet quavers are heard as pairs. This hemiola becomes increasingly used, not only in recurrences of the clarinet's idea, but for example in the 'hobbling' rhythm at fig. 7.

From here the music follows a consistent pattern, alternating passive 'interludes' with decisive steps forward. At fig. 10 we arrive at the climactic tutti, chorusing in organised confusion. Here the two principal strands of melody are combined. On the one hand is the cor anglais together with its derivative, the new figure on piccolo clarinet; on the other the 'chromatic' motif, now scored for clarinet in A. We can see now why it was so important to establish the hemiola: for at the point of maximum complexity this gives Stravinsky the option of an extra rhythmic layer. The competing strands of melody are anchored to the hemiola, whose harmony gathers the elements established earlier: the triad of E in second inversion, and as at fig. 4, again the major–minor/octatonic colouring.

What is striking is that the 'Introduction' is so 'organic'; for despite the apparently 'discontinuous' blocks, everything is geared to an evolutionary strategy. Perhaps we should not be surprised: for if the *Rite*'s sensational impact on its first listeners was due to its assault on their nervous system, the work owes its longevity to the sheer guile with which it is composed.

What happens next brutally cuts off this process of growth just as it is bursting ecstatically into bloom. The mêlée is treated as an impasse, in a way that is typical of all the great climaxes in the *Rite* with the sole exception of the problematic ending to the 'Sacrificial Dance'. Stravinsky times the cut as ruthlessly as possible, the melodies halted in mid-syllable at the point of maximum dislocation: the D clarinet, for example, is left stranded in mid-flight to the top note of its phrase. In the shocked, frozen silence the bassoon melody floats in, unmoved. Its elemental indifference, as if it had been present all along, has the effect of setting in perspective the profusion of the 'Introduction'. Yet the melody *has* moved, down a semitone: why? The short transition (figs. 12–13) which the bassoon introduces connects the 'Introduction', with its linear writing, to the starkly 'vertical' opening to 'Augurs of Spring'. With the bassoon tune transposed (now to A♭ minor), the E minor triad outlined in the original tune becomes E♭ minor. One consequence is that we again get the same minor-to-major move that we heard earlier at fig. 4, this time the minor triad 'seeding' the 'Augurs' chord itself, in the E♭ major of its upper component. The actual moment of modulation comes in the quiet chords heard just before the rise of the curtain. Before this the final note of the tune (now in A♭) has been harmonised, as earlier, by the major third, here of course C♭. This C passes, by way of clarinet and bass clarinet, down a tritone to F♯: the C/F♯ relationship then blooms in the chord on the violas (almost the *Petrushka* combination). These harmonies (C and F♯) then converge on to their mid-point – E♭, in a beautiful piece of octatonic geometry that distils the elements of the harmony to come: C/F♯ converging to E♭7, still with the minor third (F♯) held on by the bass clarinet.

This triangular relationship (C–F♯–E♭) is formed from three of the four 'nodes' of the same octatonic collection, and takes us forward to consider the harmonies of 'Augurs'. Again the basis is a triangle, three chords with notes in common. Thus at fig. 14 the chords are E major (and minor), C major and E♭7. In contrast the explosive nature of the 'Augurs' chord itself (fig. 13) (Ex. 4.4) arises from a genuine clash of tonality. For while it is possible to rationalise the F♭ as part of the same octatonic collection which gives E♭7, the same argument cannot explain the A♭ and C♭: these are 'wrong' and they sound wrong too! Given the very precise preparation (already noted) of the upper E♭7 component, the purpose and importance of the lower F♭ major triad is explicable in two ways: as an extension of the E major-centred harmony of the 'Introduction'; and as a giant accented dissonance, whose resolution – down a semitone to E♭ – will form the main, indeed only, harmonic move of 'Augurs' – at figs. 16 and 28.[2]

During the first twenty-two bars the music is anchored to the 'Augurs' harmony. If we label these bars the 'A' section, 'B' (at fig. 16) involves both the 'resolution' of the bass line, from E to E♭, and the first step away from the uncompromisingly 'vertical' rhythm to a layering of metre, with 2/4 persisting (cor anglais) but countered by the implied 3/4 of the bass line (lower strings, pizzicato).

Another sort of overlap is provided by fragments of melody. These start to form with the chromatic figure, the music of the old woman (oboe, muted trumpet after fig. 15): this outlines a tritone (B♭–E) from which an octatonic profile emerges, consistent with the interlocking of related triads we have seen earlier (before fig. 13 and at fig. 14), and consistent too (in octatonic terms) with the skittering fragment which follows on flutes and piccolos. Thus this 'B' section (from 16–18) is layered in two ways: rhythmically in the game between 2/4 and 3/4, and harmonically in the opposition between octatonic melodies and the open fifths erected in a trellis from the bass – and emphasised by the stuttering fifths on the brass.[3]

The swirling figure on the flutes and piccolos, trivial in itself, is the first appearance of the short scalar motif – the 'minor tetrachord' (T–S–T) – which will run through many of the melodies in the *Rite*. It resurfaces first at fig. 19 on bassoons just after the music has returned (at fig. 18) to the 'A' section, the stamping chords. To these the bassoons add first their own jostling accentuations (repeated B♭s), then extended, as if experimentally, into something resembling the flute/piccolo motif but a tone lower, very clearly 'in' E♭. Since the fall and rise of the tune is six quavers in length, the effect is to play teasingly across the duple rhythm. This assumes, of course, that one still hears the repeated chords as 2/4. The point is debatable since in this section the repetitions of the 'Augurs' chord are far more prolonged than at the opening (fig. 13) and the listener's sense of 2/4 may well be suspended or at least weakened – by no means the only instance in the *Rite* where Stravinsky toys with our sense of metre. At all events, the point highlights again the importance of the earlier four-bar interpolation at fig. 14 which, as we have seen, had the function of clarifying the rhythmic orientation.

A crude little canon brings this section of the movement to an impasse – and a sudden wrenching dislocation. But though jagged in terms of rhythm, Stravinsky's notes serve to reinforce the basic 'geometry' – C/F♯ again, with the E♭ harmony represented by a single unison E♭ (horns, trombones).

After this *cæsura*, the business of the movement is accumulation, as the young men, the piping *dudki* players, and the 'old woman' are joined by the young girls coming up from the river.[4] The 2/4 ostinato is fragmented, and at last removed from the long-suffering cor anglais player, while the Cs flicker into trills which have their origin in the transition after the 'Introduction'. Suddenly the whole sound-world is new – twitching, twittering, buzzing – as layers start to build. The 2/4 ostinato breaks into a canter in semiquavers, now with an upper line, G/A in alternation: marked col legno this discreetly smooths the entry of the suave horn tune (fig. 25) (Ex. 4.3j). This new building block is a little 'five-finger' tune, the upper four notes of which are identical with the flute/piccolo motif – but where that was octatonic, here the context is clearly diatonic (F major).[5]

Notice how smoothly all these gear changes are being made. One of these deftly transposes the horn melody (now for alto flute, fig. 27) so that its notes match the continuing ostinato – all that is left of the original 'Augurs' chord. This manoeuvre enables the last piece of the jigsaw to fall neatly into place, the return of the 'B' section bass (fig. 28). This final 'resolution' of the 'Augurs' chord, prefigured earlier (figs. 16–18), creates a stability of harmony within which the teasing games between 2/4 and 3/4 come to fruition. Then, overlaid as a descant to this quivering, flickering tapestry of sound, the trumpets introduce the tune of 'Spring Rounds'. Again, thanks to the ubiquitous minor tetrachord (E♭–D♭–C–B♭) this is grafted on with smooth inevitability.

This brings the music to the point where, in the original conception, it would have flowed directly into 'Spring Rounds'. But now, having switched the order of movements, so that 'Augurs' is followed by 'Ritual of Abduction', further energising transitions are required. The first of these (fig. 30) is straightforward: the 2/4 and 3/4 ostinatos continue, destabilised by agitated sequences (diminished sevenths) with a pattern of syncopations borrowed exactly from the opening of the movement. As a means of creating a sort of instant tonal crisis this is crude but effective, precipitating the most brittle and ruthless version of what was originally a 'suave' tune, now rendered hyperactive by grace notes and a marvellous orchestral effect of pizzicato in semiquavers (using up and down strokes of the plucking finger). Here in this tutti the movement comes to a crisis, a culmination of all the earlier nervous energy. As the tune compresses into a new ostinato (fig. 32), the orchestra is gripped in a ritual of highly charged panting (the sexual implication is inescapable, surely intended) capped by whooping horns.

'Ritual of Abduction' is the most terrifying of musical hunts: in purely musical terms it is a struggle to establish rhythmic coherence in the face of every disruption. The notated metre (9/8) and even the component triplets are constantly obscured, either by cross-accents or more usually by motifs whose shapes cut across the metre. An example is the first high 'fanfare' – another near-exact borrowing from *Petrushka* – which spins in groups of seven.

On the tonal plane, by contrast, 'Ritual of Abduction' is marked by stability and a return to familiar octatonic relationships, unmistakable after the whole-tone diversions at the end of 'Augurs'. Again the relationship is triangular: two overlapping complementary harmonies (E♭7 and C7) with the thudding low F♯, rhythmically an intruder but still part of the prevailing octatonic collection. The real dissonance is in the shrieking diatonic 'fanfare', which I hear as a sort of pentatonic D major (Ex. 4.3l). The octatonic geometry of the opening page is particularly neat, the F♯ at fig. 37 being answered at the tritone by C: thus F♯/C act as a hinge linking the opening C7/E♭7 harmonies with the symmetrical response (at fig. 38) on A♭7/B7.

This harmonic split defines what is almost a tiny sonata form. Its 'development' (figs. 42–3) is a rising sequence which in harmonic terms is all regularly octatonic, and regular also (at last!) in metre. The smoothness of the ascent permits a crisis of shattering rhythmic and harmonic dissonance. The 6/8 is all but shaken to bits, the tritone (F♯/C) reasserted (*più ff*) in a defiant bellow (trombones and timpani before fig. 44). Remembering the original order of the libretto, with 'Ritual of Abduction' the last but one movement in Part I, this climax would have been all the more significant, recognisable as a flashback to the opening of 'Ritual of the Rival Tribes'.[6]

A second crisis (at fig. 45) takes the form of a pincer movement: one jaw consists of superimposed diminished seventh arpeggios in a descending sequence; the other, deriving perhaps from the horns' fifths, is also a sequence, which arrives with logical inevitability on the low F at fig. 46. F is then the pivot linking this version of the 'fanfare' – cocky, triumphant almost – and the fateful ambush (at fig. 47). Here the harmony, essentially F minor–major, is the final unresolvable collision, with the tritone – C–F$\sharp$ (G$\flat$) – still very evident. These brutal chords hold the 'fanfare', now whirling round ostinato-like, in a vice-like grip.

The exit from this crisis is one of the *Rite*'s unforgettable passages. It is a moment of great stillness; yet the furious energy seems not dissipated but concentrated in the flute trills which spin at a tangent from the swirling vortices, and which deftly reveal the way forward as the trill on E$\flat$/E turns to E$\flat$/F.

The construction of the 'escape' tune (at fig. 48) (Ex. 4.3n) is beautiful in itself; and, as the transition which Stravinsky needs, it works beautifully, applying the brakes but without a trace of sentimentality. In performance it is sadly often ruined by being seen as a respite, an opportunity to indulge in 'point-making' rubato. The tune is a still voice, but as indifferent to the tumult as the bassoon solo was at the end of the 'Introduction' (fig. 12). And like the bassoon it looks back to previous pentatonic ideas, especially since its pitches and its scoring parallel the decisive move by the piccolo clarinet in the 'Introduction' (fig. 9). In the immediate past it matches also the pitches (and perhaps the F minor colouring) of the last version of the 'fanfare' (fig. 46 + 8).

As the main music of 'Spring Rounds' gets underway (fig. 49) Stravinsky deploys for the first time the mesmerising, repetitive rhythmic style which will dominate much of Part II. Anchored to a ground bass, the big tune drifts in as though sleep-walking, and with a slight vagueness in shape which causes the music occasionally to slip out of the 4/4 metre. Stillness is again the prelude to another ambush (at fig. 53) where Stravinsky releases a further line, all the more disruptive because it is a ghastly caricature of the big tune, distorting its descending steps into whole tones and its unisons into consecutive sevenths. Even the pair of rising quavers is parodied in the grotesque bray reinforced by trumpets and trombones.

Again a section ends with an impasse. The way out (Vivo, fig. 50) is a return to the music which immediately preceded 'Spring Rounds'.[7] Though a flashback to the end of 'Ritual of Abduction', there are a number of differences. The rhythmic irregularities are ironed out and with them the feeling of panic, the music now a massive reiteration, like

Ex. 5.1 First sketch for Ritual of the Rival Tribes (Sketches, p. 12)

an obstruction barring the way. Another change is in 'key', from F minor to C minor. The result is that when the quiet 'escape' melody resumes, we hear it differently, with C minor, not F minor, in our ears. The change is confirmed by the adjustment to the pitches in the tune's third bar which might otherwise have been attributed to error.

Ritual of the Rival Tribes

From the point of view of Stravinsky's working methods, the pages for 'Ritual of the Rival Tribes' are among the most revealing in the sketches for the *Rite*. They show Stravinsky shuffling the pieces of his mosaic, working by trial and error at the intractable problem of devising a continuity for his short explosive ideas. The music represents a war-game so that the ideas had to be combative, precluding the sort of continuous ostinato used in 'Augurs'. At the same time, however, the needs of the drama meant that the music had to progress, rising in tension in order to trigger the second half of the movement, the arrival of 'The Procession of the Sage'.

In the sketches Stravinsky refers to the first half of the movement as 'The Tribes'. Almost all the ideas for this spring from his very first notation. In Ex. 5.1 the two halves (A and B) are complementary:

opposed in register and (in the final score) articulation but sharing the same rolling thirds. Yet despite the obvious contrast B flows smoothly from A. The key to why this is so is a connecting melodic thread, with the upper line sharing the same (Dorian) scale. Stravinsky at once spotted the connection. His first development from the sketch[8] was to copy out a 'white-note' version of B, noting that this could be extended in an unbroken sequence a fourth higher (this gives the oddly mellifluous passage at figs. 61–2).

The realisation that the edges between blocks could be smooth as well as abrupt then governs the way Stravinsky moves his material around. One can hear this clearly in the passage between figs. 59 and 61. This begins with A (horns and tubas), repeated in a grotesque sounding transposition an octave and a major third higher (and grotesquely rescored for woodwind and violins pizzicato). The next move is a fluent one, to B (at fig. 60). B is then repeated (shortened) in an abrupt switch down the major third, a move used as a hinge, swinging the music back for the tutti reiteration of A (just before fig. 61).

After these crisp exchanges, A and B are kept apart. The sustained build-up (figs. 62–4) consists entirely of derivatives of A, chanting ferociously, and this time powered by an ostinato in the bass. B is reserved in order to represent the 'outgoing' music at the transition (figs. 64–6) where it confronts the lowing tubas which signal the advent of the Sage. As B scatters in confusion (just before fig. 66) the music builds step by step to its shattering polymetric and polymelodic climax. Against the march-time of the 'Procession' are the thuds of the bass drum marking every fourth beat, while a descant on high horns stands apart from this close rhythmic interplay, stretching out over cycles of thirteen (later seventeen) beats. Initially (at fig. 66) the tubas and bass drum work together through a three-bar cycle, extending to twelve bars (figs. 67–70) as the tubas work through three four-bar phrases. Exactly as this extended cycle is completed the tutti erupts. Here, suddenly, the competing rhythms slot into place, as each motif spins through regular cycles of fours, eights and sixteens (the march itself). Thus at the climax of Part I the same principle which climaxed the 'Introduction' in babbling confusion is here transformed, as if into some vast turbine in which every part of the mechanism moves with disciplined purpose.

The Sage

Between the disciplined fury of 'The Procession of the Sage' and the whirling vortices of 'Dance of the Earth' comes the solemn moment when the wise elder kisses the earth. The musical representation is terse, even laconic. The sound is bleached free of colour: bassoons (with basses and timpani) sketch the Sage's shuffling movement while the kiss itself is a glassy chord (string harmonics). Rather like the transition at the end of the 'Introduction', the quietness allows Stravinsky to sow seeds, to scrutinise intervals in his microscope. The harmony, of overlapping thirds, opens the way for the tumbling thirds of 'Dance of the Earth', while the C minor colouring of the chord makes this a protracted inward breath which is released in the random C major 'shouts' that follow. Looking further ahead, the B♭/C harmonies anticipate the duet for trumpets (fig. 86), hence the underlying motif which recurs throughout Part II.

Dance of the Earth

The music of 'Dance of the Earth' stems entirely from two melodies inscribed on the sketches (Ex. 5.2).[9] This does not mean, however, that its ideas have no connection with what has gone before. The first two bars – a sort of anacrusis – spring up from the bass drum which has been so prominent in the 'meltdown' at the end of 'Procession of the Sage'. The tumbling thirds, though coming from the folk source, look back to the thirds in 'Ritual of the Rival Tribes'. Also familiar are the punched chords, similar, for example, to the crisis before 'Spring Rounds'. Lastly there is the fact that the bass ostinato pivots around the tritone F♯/C, so frequently employed already as an octatonic 'hinge'.

The thrilling fanfare-like thirds in the upper part of the orchestra inhabit the C major of the source tune, together with its distinctive push upwards through whole tones (F♯, G♯). It is this distinctive whole-tone feature of the source melody which Stravinsky extracts to create the bass ostinato – which rotates a whole-tone scale against the low C and stokes Stravinsky's imagined 'prairie-fire'.[10] Tonally, therefore, it is C (in the upper part of the orchestra) which is set against F♯, implied by the three-note ostinato – the *Petrushka* combination again.

Ex. 5.2 Source melodies for Dance of the Earth (Sketches, p. 35)

(a)

(b)

Then at the mid-point of the dance – *piano subito* (fig. 75) – we meet again the third 'node' of the octatonic triangle: E♭. Here the horns and violas begin their hunting triplets (another glance backwards, this time to 'Ritual of Abduction') using the notes of the minor tetrachord (here E♭ D♭ C B♭). The game of F♯ versus C continues as the whole-tone ostinato stretches upwards to encompass the remaining (white) notes necessary to complete the scale: C D E. The final strand, in semiquavers on the violins, is particularly ingenious. In one sense it adds a new octatonic dimension, 'foreign' to the C/F♯/E♭ triangle already in play. In another sense it is perfectly smooth and logical, since the violins' tetrachord is a perfect fifth above the tetrachord used by the horns. We have already seen Stravinsky building up layers in fifths, in the 'trellis' in 'Augurs', for example. Now the effect is of a fugato as overlapping entries rise like fugal subjects, answering one another at the fifth then the octave and climbing again, another fifth higher, at fig. 76 + 4.

Rhythmically something is new. We have met earlier, in the big tune of 'Spring Rounds', a melody flowing out of repeated notes. There the number of repetitions was subtly varied, with the effect of slightly destabilising the metre. Here that simple trick is carried to the limit. The effect is to produce a new kind of polymetric layering, which works as follows. There are three layers: the bass ostinato, in quavers; the horns in triplets; the trumpets in semiquavers. All are tied, naturally, to the same (crotchet) beat. But whereas the ear is educated to hear the bass ostinato in a regular 3/4 metre, the metric grouping of the upper two lines is dependent always on how many repeated notes Stravinsky chooses to use, something which is perpetually unforeseeable. As a result, 'Dance of the Earth' is a first foretaste of the great metrical storms of Part II; and the use of unpredictable numbers of repetitions looks forward specifically to the role of the 'vamp' in 'Glorification of the Chosen One'.

All this sounds exciting. So too is the fact that in 'Dance of the Earth' Stravinsky's most far-reaching innovations are so closely tied to tradition.[11] And yet I have to say that this is the one passage in the *Rite* which seems more manufactured than inspired. Partly it is the fault of the harmonies, which for all the ingenious dovetailing of diatonic, octatonic and whole tone, just spin round, expending furious amounts of energy running on the spot. And perhaps the rhythms are too complicated, too unpredictable, so that – at this necessarily headlong tempo – the ear gives up the effort of 'predicting' and accepts the music simply as a complex effect.

There is, finally, the problem of how to end. Originally Stravinsky planned to add a sostenuto chord to glue the final bars together.[12] Why did he abandon the idea? Partly perhaps, on musical grounds, because the pitches of the chord would have interfered with the balance of layers already described.[13] But mostly, I suspect, because such an ending would have compromised the very spirit of the *Rite*, whereby ideas are unceasing: they are felt to continue even when they have been made to disappear, as for example we sense when the bassoon melody returns at the end of the 'Introduction'. The moment at which something stops must therefore be made to appear arbitrary. This is always carefully contrived, of course. And here the dramatist in Stravinsky cannot resist a final tightening of the screw, as the bass ostinato fights its way up into the heart of the conflagration by way of adding a second octave to the whole-tone scale. Nonetheless it is interesting to observe Stravinsky aware of the problem of how to end – shelved for the time being – and falling back, wisely, on the blunt, brutal amputation – another cliffhanger – which so far had served so well.

Part II

The music of Part I has been fast, brilliant, violent. Now as 'Day' turns to 'Night' and the plot on stage thickens, Stravinsky's music moves to an altogether deeper level of coherence.

The way this is done may come as a surprise. Far from being 'non-linear', as it is usually described, the music traces an inexorable arc of development which stretches from the first notes of the 'Introduction' to the end of the 'Sacrificial Dance' (Exx. 5.3–10). This has its origins (in Part II's 'Introduction') in two distinct groups or 'waves' of ideas. Among these is a tune which, when the curtain eventually rises, is revealed as the folk-like khorovod which accompanies the young girls ('Mystic Circles'). The tune is answered by another, closely related, also folk-like; this however disperses rapidly as a shiver runs through the music. Stravinsky's response to this impasse is revealing – a structural 'window', with a flashback which reconnects the music with the underlying continuity, by returning (in varied form) to the two main ideas of the 'Introduction'. This passage acts as a prelude which enables the first tune of 'Mystic Circles' to return, in further versions which accompany the fateful ritual in which the young girls choose the sacrificial victim by lot.

Once the die is cast the music erupts in orgiastic celebration – 'The Glorification of the Chosen One'. For the first time the basic continuity is broken, the dance being a fierce interruption, rather analogous to the position of 'Ritual of Abduction' in the structure of Part I. (We will see, however, how securely Stravinsky anchors this section to the surrounding structure.) The music returns to the main path at 'Ritual Action of the Ancestors', and does so with a vengeance: this will be a melting-pot in which all the main musical motifs simultaneously come to a head – a point in favour of the hypothesis, advanced earlier, that this was originally envisaged as the *Rite*'s final movement. Lastly the 'Sacrificial Dance', though in a sense standing apart as a final 'set-piece', is also closely integrated with the rest of Part II – hardly surprising since (as we saw in the sketches) Stravinsky borrowed its material for the 'Introduction'.

In discussing the music as it appears in the finished score we have the benefit of hindsight. How conscious was Stravinsky of this emerging evolution? Probably not until well into the sketches for Part II, though certainly it seems part of a deliberate strategy by the time he came to compose 'Ritual Action'. When he came to write the 'Introduction' – which he did only after composing the rest of Part II – there is no doubt that he saw its function as establishing a seedbed of ideas.

The black sonority which opens Part II manages to be both still and expectant, profound but unstable (Ex. 5.3). The enveloping harmony is a chord of D minor, pinned dissonantly by woodwind triads which oscillate between the semitones on either side (E♭ minor and C♯ minor). Stravinsky's first move (at the end of bar 2) is to push the harmony upwards as if seeking escape, into a rich configuration which is recognisably octatonic, with the underlying harmony moving from D minor to E7: a detail which will become an important feature is the clash of G with the major third (G♯) of the E7 chord. Hence what we hear is a sort of modulation, from tonal to octatonic[14] and from a closed to a more open and 'hopeful' sound. Though decisive, the progression is 'hinged' – thanks to pitches common to both harmonies: the D, and the falling melodic tritone, B♭–E, so that the music slips readily back to its starting-point. This beautiful piece of geometry (the 'push' motif) will be the core idea of Part II.[15] Exx. 5.3–5.10 contain ideas from Part II which illustrate the push towards the end of the phrase.

Progress at first is almost painfully deliberate. But as the upper harmonies start to stray a descant emerges at fig. 80 + 3 which, as it acquires a melodic shape, becomes a premonition of the maidens' khorovod ('Mystic Circles'). Its harmonisation is important: combined with the D minor–E 7 progression (of the 'push' motif) the tune too seems to push forwards, towards its final two notes – thanks to the major–minor clash (again G♯/G♮, as already noted in bar 2) which will be one of the characteristic sonorities of Part II (fig. 81 + 3). Then at last there is a third, and this time successful, attempt to modulate (figs. 82–3). Once again octatonic harmony (as in bar 2) is the springboard, swelling this time into a rich Skryabin-like sequence which, as we have seen from the sketches, is modelled on a passage from the 'Sacrificial Dance' (Ex. 2.5).

As the music breaks free to a new tonality (F♯ replacing D), the melody too is on the move, hesitating and circling (from fig. 83). This new flexibility is also applied to the lower layer of harmony: in place of the former 'rootedness' (as at fig. 81) the new tonic triad of F♯ minor is in its first inversion, so that the 'push' to G♯7 is more like a sideslip, further smoothed by the suspension (C♯ falling to B♯: fig. 83 + 2). This eloquence is no passing accident: Stravinsky is carefully steering the

Ex. 5.3 Introduction (to Part II)

Ex. 5.4 Introduction

Ex. 5.5 Introduction

Ex. 5.6 Mystic Circles of the Young Girls

Ex. 5.7 Mystic Circles of the Young Girls

Ex. 5.8 Ritual Action of the Ancestors

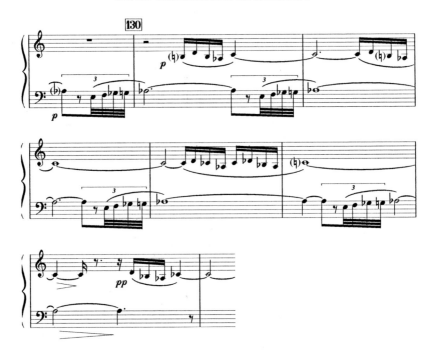

descant-tune towards the rich chromatic character it will acquire when the curtain rises.

We have now reached the connecting passage inserted in March 1913. In line with previous transitions, the 'outgoing' music starts to falter, opening a gap into which the 'incoming' insinuates itself. The way this is done is highly significant since it reveals that Stravinsky now understood, as he had not done earlier, the central role of the 'push'

Ex. 5.9 Ritual Action of the Ancestors

Ex. 5.10 Sacrificial Dance

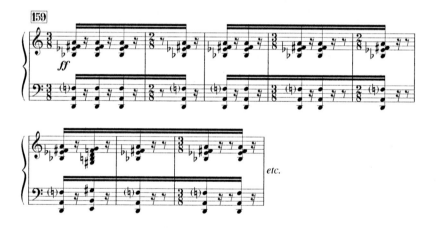

motif in the structure of Part II. First he breaks up the descant–tune by
isolating its initial three notes (fig. 84 + 3). This fragment is further
reduced (at fig. 85), a moment of particular significance since it is a
pre-echo of the fatal 'tocsin', the moment at the end of 'Mystic Circles'
when the sacrificial victim is chosen. Before this, almost unnoticed, the
music has slipped into the lush harmonies which will lead 'Mystic
Circles' (at fig. 91) to its fateful destiny. Originally Stravinsky sketched
this beginning on a chord of F♯7, as a smooth continuation from the

preceding F♯ minor. Now, by transposing the music to B♭ he adds another logical tonal step (in the sequence D–F♯–B♭); but at the same time he prepares the arrival of the duet for two trumpets with the 'charm' motif[16] which will begin the second phase of the 'Introduction' at fig. 86. Within the context Stravinsky has now engineered, this duet is heard as outlining a harmony of B♭7, which then pushes outwards to C/E♮. The inference is clear: this new idea has the same pattern as the 'push' motif – oscillations which veer outwards on the last beat of the phrase; and the similarity extends to the harmony, which makes the same move, up a tone.

When the trumpets resume at fig. 86, their syncopations tense and flex hypnotically (Ex. 5.5). The stillness and remoteness make the duet an exercise in suspense: the music here is quieter than anything heard since the opening bassoon solo. The passage gives an interesting insight into the way Stravinsky co-ordinates independent blocks of rhythm. The lower instruments creeping in are fragmentary and disruptive, like ice creaking ominously, sketching incidentally another form of the 'push'. But they have to give precedence to the pacing of the duet, Stravinsky compressing their rhythm, shoehorning it into place for the sake of preserving the regularity of the 5/4 metre.

We expect something to happen, and it does – in a heart-stopping shock (upbeat to fig. 87), as C7, long implied, blooms suddenly. The preparatory tracing (from fig. 86) is now realised in three layers. The bass pizzicati, a four-note ostinato rhythmically disrupted, support the oscillation in the upper strands between major–minor chords (as expected, on B♭7 and C7); the third layer is the trumpets' duet, glowing dully on horns and clarinets.

The 'Introduction' reaches an impasse, very similar to the tutti at the end of the 'Introduction' to Part I. And as in Part I the way out is simple and ruthless, an abrupt cut-off, with only a trail of C major (flute harmonics) allowed to linger. Meanwhile – another similarity – a transition prepares the rise of the curtain. This Stravinsky does by restating two of the main ideas of the 'Introduction', juxtaposed so as to emphasise their differences: the 'Mystic Circles' melody (scored naively, even wistfully) and the duet, now in a Stygian sonority.

Mystic Circles

As the curtain rises the theme of 'Mystic Circles', long prepared, moves centre-stage (Ex. 5.6). The step is striking, from the growling depths to this treble sonority with its clear tonality (there is even a key signature: B major) and light scoring for solo strings. But the effect, anything but light, seems more like a grotesque parody of the innocent khorovods of *Firebird*. What should be an artless tune is curdled by the semitonal puns of the harmonisation. This game between clashing major and minor thirds (or between triads and diminished triads) has a saccharine sweetness, the somnabulistic repetitions of the melody tainted with corruption. Also disconcerting is the oddly metronomic counterpoint in the cellos, in a metre of its own (2/4) and sempre staccato against the glutinous legato of the upper strings: if nothing else it ensures that the tune is played senza rubato.

One upshot of the semitonal uncertainties is that the chord which halts this opening statement sounds unexpectedly 'clean': this will be the magic chord, the 'tocsin', which will return at the end of 'Mystic Circles', just before the slithering avalanche which precipitates 'Glorification of the Chosen One'. Here the reaction is an unmistakable *frisson*, shivering through the trill for clarinet (fig. 93). The trill introduces a melody for alto flute (Ex. 4.3s) which sounds like a derivative of the main theme of 'Mystic Circles'.[17] This subsidiary tune is then fractured into segments under pressure from the inner tremolos and the excruciating doubling of the tune at the seventh. The answer to this spiral of terror is (true to type) deadpan, and – in terms of the continuity so patiently and powerfully established in the 'Introduction' – absolutely consistent. Once again the music picks up the underlying thread. At first we might not recognise this, in the strange ostinato (fig. 97) in which the arrangement of pitches stifles resonance so that the sound is reduced to a percussive thud. But these pitches (D♯[E♭]/C♯) are chosen deliberately, as representatives of the triads of E♭ minor and C♯ minor which opened the 'Introduction', reduced here to bare bones. Sure enough the harmony on D floats in, also weirdly skeletal, in open fifths (A–D), and pushing into the parallel sevenths (at fig. 97 + 4 and + 6) for which the ear has been prepared by the earlier excruciating descant to the source melody (Ex. 5.7). At fig. 98 the open fifth climbs to an insistent falling fourth (D–A): both pitches have become 'minor thirds' grinding against lower dominant seventh harmonies on B and F♯. Again the musical idea is the 'push' motif, stretching convulsively to the final minim of the bar. All these factors make this transition a summary, redefining the steps which in the 'Introduction' led the opening music to 'Mystic Circles'.

The decisive moment in the libretto, the choosing of the sacrificial victim, has arrived. The maidens resume their circling at fig. 99. This time, however, their melody has a different colouring, in a harmonisation which is intense and chromatic. Again the 'push' is in evidence, with the major–minor clash (A♯/A♮: the underlying harmony is on F♯) on the last (minim) beat of each phrase.

In terms of the drama, this is a deadly game of pass-the-parcel: if the music stops on you, you are 'it', the chosen victim. The decisive interruption is the 'tocsin' which comes a bar before fig. 102, as the accompanying stage direction in the four-hand piano score, but not in the orchestral score, makes clear – 'The dance stops. One of the young girls is chosen by lot for the sacrifice.'[18] At once the horns, in alternation, clarify and underline the chord. As the music hurtles towards the precipice the harmony splinters apart, into what Stravinsky would later call the 'orchestral haemorrhage',[19] the moment of catastrophe marked by the 'shriek' with which the orchestra disperses (presumably the Maidens also) before re-forming in the hammered crotchets of the 11/4 bar, with strings (ben marcato e pesante) and a quartet of timpani with bass drum.

Glorification of the Chosen One

This ferociously exultant or (as Stravinsky originally conceived it) 'Amazonian' dance[20] has parallels with the 'Ritual of Abduction'. Both are stunning, savage interruptions; and in both there is a simplification in harmony, here for the most part straightforwardly octatonic – perhaps because of the music's emphasis on 'raw' rhythm. In 'Glorification' the chords formed in the upper parts are almost exclusively 'quartal': that is, three-note chords consisting of a perfect and augmented fourth. The first of these 'fourths' chords (of exactly the type heard earlier in the 'Introduction', figs. 87–9) is heard at a point of maximum emphasis, at the top of the uprushing 'shriek'. And of course the chords of the 11/4 bar are also 'fourths' chords, a symmetrical pair which overlap. Played on the piano (as in the *seconda* part of the four-hand version) the pianist's thumbs interlock; one can imagine Stravinsky discovering this sound, gleefully pounding these chords on the muted upright piano in his tiny studio at Clarens.

Taken together, the 'shriek' and the colossal emphasis of the 11/4 bar establish the upbeat-downbeat shape of the main idea of 'Glorification'. Originally – in the sketches – Stravinsky envisaged underlining the connection by having the 11/4 bar and the opening of 'Glorification' at the same tempo.

The sketches also make clear the sense of the rhythm. We are supposed to hear the 5/8 bar (at 104) as 3 + 2 (Ex. 4.16). The shape of the melody (up/down) confirms this; so too does the harmony, with the chord on the second beat a dissonance – thanks to the G♯ (which is foreign to the prevailing octatonic collection) which 'resolves' on the fourth quaver. Both counter the tendency for the ear to follow the bass line (with the timpani whacks on the first and third quavers) as the beat – in which case the bar would sound as 2 + 3. It is important also that we hear the subsequent 9/8 bar not as three regular dotted crotchet beats but as a crude duple-time 'vamp' (as Taruskin describes it) alternating between, as it were, Stravinsky's left and right hands.[21]

One of Stravinsky's inspired decisions was to make the hammered 'fourths' chords of the 11/4 bar (together with the 'shriek') an integral idea within the dance and not just a preparatory gesture. The music juggles four ideas: the music of the first bar; the 'vamp'; the 'reverse vamp' which has the stress on the upper chord, or 'right hand'; and the uprushing scales. The jagged interplay is similar in principle to the 'Sacrificial Dance'; but here the effect is more fluid, more anarchically wild, where the 'Sacrificial Dance' is inexorable. Part of the reason is in the impetuous aggression of the uprushing scales which each time elbow in earlier than they should.

The central section of 'Glorification' (figs. 111–17) is a development of the vamp, with 'fourths' chords in spiky syncopations. Then at the recapitulation (of the first section) with which 'Glorification' ends, Stravinsky completely omits the 'reverse vamp', while the uprushing scales are confined to a single upbeat used as a launch-pad (see fig. 117).

Ex. 5.11 Evocation of the Ancestors

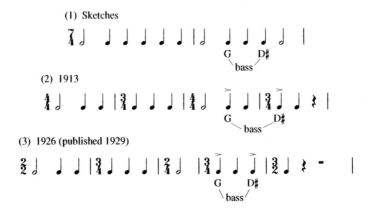

(1) Sketches

(2) 1913

(3) 1926 (published 1929)

Other than this the recapitulation is an identical copy of the opening section.

Evocation of the Ancestors

'Glorification' ends, as it began, with an overlap. The bass motif which so dramatically announces 'Evocation' – biting hard as the music seems to fight for grip – is clearly the main melodic idea of 'Glorification'. With D♯ in the bass and the unmistakable C major of the chordal blocks, the major–minor sonority is brought to a blazing climax in this great wind and brass fanfare. Meanwhile, though perhaps less obviously, the duple-versus-triple rhythm derives also from 'Glorification' (the fist-shaking on trumpets and trombones at fig. 115 + 2) – in the first sketch this was originally in even note values.[22]

'Evocation' achieves a massive authority, but remains rhythmically light on its feet. The secret is in the extreme instability of metre, whose notation caused Stravinsky endless trouble, as we can see in the steps from sketch to finished score and later revisions (Ex. 5.11). Originally the opening two bars of the fanfare were sketched as a single bar of 7/4, in line with Stravinsky's practice at that time of barring according to the phrase. Next he decided to divide this bar into two, the division coinciding with the change in harmony – possibly, also, on the grounds that having two segments of 4 + 3, which the conductor could therefore initiate with a minim upbeat, would be easier to perform.[23]

Whatever the reason, the resulting triple metre at fig. 121 + 5 became not just a notational convenience, but a rhythmic motif in its own right. Eventually this motif reappeared at the end of the phrase, so that the last four chords (fig. 121 + 7) become a 3/4 bar plus a downbeat. No doubt Stravinsky was worried that this 3/4 barring would seem perverse, given the plainly duple implication of the clinching accents and the move in the bass back to D♯. All the evidence in the *Rite* points to the fact that Stravinsky was scrupulous in matters of notation, well aware that it is one thing to write a syncopation, quite another to hear it as such – hence the carefully engineered context for the irregular accents which open 'Augurs of Spring', and those found later at the start of 'Sacrificial Dance'.

Perhaps the problem was simply insoluble, since no one system of barring could express all the rhythm in all its aspects. But in the end there seem to be sufficient reasons to end the phrase in question with a 3/4 metre (fig. 121 + 7). Throughout 'Evocation' metre combines with harmonic movement to form patterns which are consistent – unvaryingly so: again the idea depends upon discrete segments or 'cells'. The rules of the game are as follows: all phrases start with a chord of C6, and all begin on the downbeat; all C6 chords longer than a crotchet (and this definition includes the last chords of phrases) are downbeats; and most importantly, the first move to C9 in each phrase is always a downbeat, and always the first beat of a triple metre. (The game between duple and triple metre is particularly piquant in the *piano* passages for bassoons from fig. 125.) Given these three 'rules', the ear readily accepts a basic pulse of minims, varied by addition (to a 3/4 bar) – with fig. 121 + 7 being a rhythmic ambiguity of the sort discussed in the first bar of 'Glorification'. Finally, a small but telling detail: the fact that the last chord of this bar is an accented syncopation (off rather than on the beat) – and assuming it is perceived as such – gives just an ounce more emphasis to Stravinsky's decision to regain and reiterate the bass D♯ at the point of maximum dissonance.[24]

Ritual Action of the Ancestors

The pay-off from these disturbances of stress and metre comes in the subsequent plunge into an ostinato of metronomic quavers. The harmony tentatively traces the notes of Stravinsky's 'dark' triad (E♭ minor plus ninth), the harmony of 'Spring Rounds', and in more recent memory the notes of the Stygian passage (at fig. 90) which immediately preceded 'Mystic Circles'.

Piece by piece the music assembles, first with the cor anglais rasping chromatically upwards then joined by the self-absorbed curling tracery of the alto flute in its lowest register – an obvious echo of Rimskyan orientalism, but as with the theme of 'Mystic Circles' denied any self-indulgence by the remorseless thud of the ostinato. The notes sound familiar – the E/A♭ of the chromatic slither and the vacillation between C♭ and C♮ on the flute; and indeed they are, being nothing less than the trumpets' duet picked apart and re-assembled (Ex. 5.8). In order to clarify the connection with the trumpets this example is based on the notation of the four-hand score.

The line fragments, left uncomfortably 'in the air' on C♭; but after a bar's rest the flute resumes, climbing a notch to start on C♯ (bypassing the expected C♮) so that its octatonic meanderings conform with the D/B♭ ostinato. This is now renewed in a pungent scoring which includes bassoons and cor anglais, and which carries forward the 'push' motif in halting accented dissonances (fig. 131 + 3,4). Not for the first time an increase in tension has been signalled by a rise of a semitone.

The tune on trumpets which now floats in (at fig. 132) is a new idea but feels familiar. For though derived from its own source-melody (as we have seen in the sketches), it too probes the intervals of the minor tetrachord (tone–semitone–tone) common to so many of the *Rite*'s melodies, most recently those of 'Mystic Circles' and its subsidiary (the alto flute after fig. 93). A point of contact between the three strands – the alto flute, the ostinato, the trumpets – is made each time the flute touches on the upper F. Stravinsky evidently attached great importance to this exquisite colouring, placing it (with a single exception) on the last crotchet beat of the bar – another manifestation of the off-centre 'push' motif (Ex. 5.9).[25]

Stealthily, piece by piece, the forces are being manoeuvred into place.

Again the music rebuilds: first the flute is doubled at the upper octave (fig. 133) while upper tremolos, initially just flecks of colour, solidify into the 'charm' motif (here all but exact – though, of course, because of the flute's shift up a semitone at fig. 131, a semitone up on the original and its cor anglais/alto flute variant at fig. 130). Without warning the first climax is suddenly, shatteringly, unleashed. The minor-tetrachord theme exults, against a counterpoint of zig-zagging fourths (C♯–G♯, B–F♯ B♭–F).

This first triumph of this theme and its tonality of C♯ is permitted only a single statement. At once the screw tightens as before (at fig. 131), with a semitonal shift upwards from C♯ to D (fig. 135). The idea which follows, however, is the 'push' in reverse, this time lurching down from D to C♯, a sort of grunt followed by a despairing bellow. Meanwhile more motifs are flying home. One is the falling slither (A to E♯), the retrograde, a semitone higher, of the earlier slither (after fig. 129): this is part of the triangle of pitches (F♯/A/E♯) which correspond to the last three notes of the lower line of the trumpets' 'charm' motif.[26]

By now all pretence at stealth has been abandoned. The music cranks up through the gears, the 'grunt' restarting not a semitone but a major third higher (in line with the sequence-building engineered in Part II's 'Introduction'). The whole passage (figs. 135–8) seems exasperated to the point of distraction. Its goal is the cataclysmic second climax of the minor-tetrachord theme, transformed again so that its features are massively emphasised – the high horns, played *pavillons en l'air* – having a barbaric splendour matching their role in the 'Procession of the Sage'. The harmony, meanwhile, distils the *Rite*'s essential sonority: the basses touch bottom on the lowest open C, supporting a trellis of open fifths (C–G–D), from which arises the 'fourths' chord (derived [G, D] B♭–F–B♭) with its major–minor clash. Meanwhile what was the undulation on alto flute (C♯, D, E, F) screams overhead on the E♭ clarinet.

As always in the *Rite*, there is no graded descent from the summit. With a flick of a switch the tutti is extinguished: we are back where we started, exactly as if nothing had happened, with the implacable ostinato (as at fig. 129), the slither and the alto flute.

What follows was intended (as we have seen) as the work's ending, but becomes now the *Rite*'s last (and most spellbinding) transition. The flute's line is taken over by a clarinet and climbs a semitone once again (to D♭), its oscillations doubled by a bass clarinet so that the handover from treble to bass is seamless. Tentative, fluttering oscillations (D♭/ C♭) glance backwards (at the minor-tetrachord theme) while arpeggiations trace the familiar C and B♭ minor/major harmonies (see fig. 140 + 2 and fig. 141 + 3,4). Meanwhile the inexorable ostinato starts to falter, dissolved by the improvisatory acrobatics of the bass clarinets and by silences. This transition differs from its predecessors in that for the first time the gaps are left unfilled.

The crucial point for orchestra and conductor (and composer) is the chord at fig. 142 which decisively announces the 'Sacrificial Dance'. Both as an eruptive gesture – and because of the sense of what follows – it must be heard as it is written, as a syncopation. Stravinsky in a sense gambles with our ability to hold on to the location of the beat, ingrained in us since fig. 129; but equally the sense of the passage requires implacable performance – in particular the final septuplet (*perdendosi*) on the bass clarinet must not be rushed.

Sacrificial Dance

These first five bars of the 'Sacrificial Dance' were Stravinsky's initial idea . Rhythmically these jagged slashes are viciously unstable – they might be described as a series of syncopations desperately seeking a downbeat. The first chords have a 'kick' equal to the visceral down bows at the start of 'Augurs'; and on close inspection they prove to be similar in their structure, perhaps deliberately so.

The E♭ at the bottom of the first chord transfers upwards to form a cluster with D and C♯. This is not arbitrary – merely a way of making the dissonance sharper – but can be traced back plausibly to the D plus E♭/C♯ from the first bars of Part II. Equally the way the harmony develops emphasises the way D is pinned symmetrically by C♯ and E♭, thanks to the tailpiece of three semiquaver chords which pivot around C♯ 7, and the 'answer' (at 144) which pounds out E♭ minor. This intrusive bar is a foretaste of the clashing cells which will govern the final section of the 'Sacrificial Dance' (from fig. 186).

The opening passage (figs. 142–9) proves to be the exposition of a ternary (A–B–A) structure. The middle section, B, is a contrast on all

counts. Tense and taut but still, the only movement is in the metronomic tick of the rhythmic cells as they explore every permutation of
their pattern. Across this, the cluster of semitones finds a new role in the
trombone's jagged quintuplet.

As in 'Ritual Action', each turn of the screw is marked by a tightening
of the harmony. The climax comes (at fig. 159) in a massive harmony on
D with clashing F/F♯. From this springboard – in which are distilled all
the fundamental sonorities of Part II, if not of the *Rite* as a whole – the
music concertinas forward and back, hinging on a central harmony of E9
plus G♮ (Ex. 5.10): in other words we are back with the 'push' idea, and
in precisely the D minor/E major harmonies of the first line of the
'Introduction'.

Abruptly (fig. 162) the music of the rhythmic cells which opened the
section resumes, a tone lower, initiating a transition which turns out to
be a carefully contrived tonal manœuvre, careful enough for the ensuing
switch in tonality not to seem the wrench it might have been. For what
follows is a literal da capo of the 'Sacrificial Dance's' first section, but
this time a semitone lower, in what Stravinsky (in the sketches) referred
to as 'C♯ major'.[27] Why C♯? Because the switch in tonality is a neat
solution to Stravinsky's long-term strategy. Given his solution of building the closing pages on the dominant (A), preceded by a sort of heroic
reassertion of D (from fig. 174), C♯ is the ideal springboard: a further
section at this point in the 'tonic' would rob later climaxes of their force.
Furthermore, like almost everything in the *Rite*, the move is based on
painstakingly established precedent, with C♯ consistently used as a
satellite of D.

The A–B–A structure has run its course by fig. 174. The first coda,
from here to fig. 186, is one of the *Rite*'s wildest patches: indeed it seems
as if Part II will end in much the same way as Part I. The huge
percussion section is at last in full cry, turbulent and self-absorbed, so
that melodic fragments hover like descants above this stampede. Always
D is the plumb-line, the tune (marcato) dips and climbs symmetrically
around this in steps of whole tones – another parallel with the 'Dance of
the Earth'.

For a moment the music feints as if to restart the 'Sacrificial Dance'
(fig. 180). This flashback is another move in Stravinsky's endgame: it is
both a *cæsura* – a momentary catching of the breath from which the

storm resumes with even greater fury – and a 'window' which renews contact with the opening music of the 'Sacrificial Dance', for reasons which will shortly become apparent.

Stravinsky's key decision was to conclude Part II not with a sort of orgy that ends Part I ('Dance of the Earth') but with a disciplined 'ritual', a forerunner of rituals in *Les Noces*, *Apollo* or *Symphony of Psalms*. Thus at fig. 186 the music suddenly becomes taut, expectant, purposeful – 'vertical', not linear. This is the music of the opening section (signposted by the flashback at fig. 180) but now segmented into a pair of short cells and transposed from D to the dominant A. Earlier (see Chapter 4, pp. 57–9), I described the way this music drives to the line, with an inexorable accumulation, halted by the *Rite*'s final impasse (fig. 201). This impasse forms the anacrusis, the pinnacle of tension resolved by the cadence onto the final D-centred chord.

The surest way to find how a piece of music works is to study its end. Hitherto the great impasses of the *Rite* have been stopped dead in their tracks, ruthlessly amputated, usually at the point of maximum dislocation. But the 'Sacrificial Dance' is the final section: it cannot merely stop, it must finish. For the first and only time, the issue cannot be evaded.

Stravinsky was not alone in finding the end a disappointment. Hostile critics were quick to seize on this one moment of weakness. Cecil Gray, writing in the 1920s, likened the music to a top or gyroscope which 'in the last bars of the work ... suddenly falls over on its side with a lurch...'[28] For Benois it was the timing that was unconvincing: 'Perhaps the ending is too abrupt?', he asked.[29]

For Stravinsky the problem was in the final chord – 'a noise'.[30] Stravinsky never found a satisfactory solution. Perhaps there never could be one. For the slight anticlimax at the end is not a matter of momentary misjudgement, which might be cured with a little tinkering. The essence of the whole work is involved, a music which is exciting yet dispassionate, exciting *because* dispassionate. Ideas are set against one another on a collision course, and the result is a music whose energy and ferocity were without precedent, and have never been surpassed. But as they collide, the ideas never once give way. 'Resolution' is simply not in the music's nature.

Of course, the end of the work is entirely different in its effect in the theatre: with the spectacle of a dancer collapsing from a real, as well as feigned, exhaustion, the music's expiration is a vivid embodiment of what is happening on stage. Its very abruptness makes you catch your breath, so that you gasp, not clap – in its proper setting this is a *coup de théâtre* of extraordinary brilliance. Here, perhaps more than anywhere else in the *Rite*, the music needs to be experienced in the way it was originally meant – as a ballet, a dramatic narrative rather than the 'abstraction' Stravinsky later preferred.

Part III

Aftermath

6

Anthology

Pierre Lalo, 'Le Temps', 5 August 1913, in 'Dossier de Presse',
pp. 33–4

This characteristic, which imposes itself aggressively on the attention, is that this is the most dissonant music ever written. I would say, after a first and very imperfect hearing, that never has the system and cult of the wrong note been practised with such zeal and persistence as in this score; that from the first bar to the last whatever note one expects is never the one that comes, but the note to one side, the note which ought not to come; that whatever chord is suggested by the previous harmony, it is always another which arrives, and that this chord and this note produce most often the effect of acute and almost cruel falseness ... the music is rough and violent, animated by an inner energy revealed in sharp and powerful rhythms, in the intense colour and brilliant richness of the orchestration, and finally in the harmonies, which have excited so much disgust and so much enthusiasm. These are not pretty, elegant harmonies, combined with patient subtlety. They are hard, loud, dense, freely invented by a cruel and fertile musical nature. This music has nothing in common with the most recent music of other composers ... and its influence should be salutary: for it would assist powerfully in destroying the cult of the seductive chord and the precious harmony which for too many years has made our art insipid ...

Igor Stravinsky, 'Montjoie!' 29 May 1913, in 'Dossier de Presse',
pp. 13–15; trans. from 'Pictures and Documents', pp. 524–6

In 'The Consecration of Spring' I wished to express the sublime uprising of Nature renewing herself – the whole pantheistic uprising of the universal harvest.

In the Prelude, before the curtain rises, I have confided to my orchestra the great fear which weighs on every sensitive soul confronted with potentialities, the 'thing in one's self', which may increase and develop infinitely. A feeble flute tone may contain potentiality, spreading throughout the orchestra. It is the obscure and immense sensation of which all things are conscious when Nature renews its forms; it is the vague and profound uneasiness of a universal puberty. Even in my orchestration and my melodic development I have sought to define it.

The whole Prelude is based upon a continuous 'mezzo forte'. The melody develops in a horizontal line that only masses of instruments (the intense dynamic power of the orchestra and not the melodic line itself) increase or diminish. In consequence, I have not given this melody to the strings, which are too symbolic and representative of the human voice; with the crescendi and diminuendi, I have brought forward the wind instruments which have a drier tone, which are more precise, less endowed with facile expression, and on this account more suitable for my purpose.

In short, I have tried to express in this Prelude the fear of nature before the arising of beauty, a sacred terror at the midday sun, a sort of pagan cry. The musical material itself swells, enlarges, expands. Each instrument is like a bud which grows on the bark of an aged tree; it becomes part of an imposing whole. And the whole orchestra, all this massing of instruments, should have the significance of the Birth of Spring.

In the first scene, some adolescent boys appear with a very old woman, whose age and even whose century is unknown, who knows the secrets of nature, and teaches her sons Prediction. She runs, bent over the earth, half-woman, half-beast. The adolescents at her side are Augurs of Spring, who mark in their steps the rhythm of spring, the pulse-beat of spring.

During this time the adolescent girls come from the river. They form a circle which mingles with the boys' circle. They are not entirely formed beings; their sex is single and double like that of the tree. The groups mingle, but in their rhythms one feels the cataclysm of groups about to form. In fact they divide right and left. It is the realization of form, the synthesis of rhythms, and the thing formed produces a new rhythm.

The groups separate and compete, messengers come from one to the other and they quarrel. It is the defining of forces through struggle, that is to say through games. But a Procession arrives. It is the Saint, the Sage, the Pontifex, the oldest of the clan. All are seized with terror. The Sage gives a benediction to the Earth, stretched flat, his arms and legs stretched out, becoming one with the soil. His benediction is as a signal for an eruption of rhythm. Each, covering his head, runs in spirals, pouring forth in numbers, like the new energies of nature. It is the Dance of the Earth.

The second scene begins with an obscure game of the adolescent girls. At the beginning, a musical picture is based upon a song which accompanies the young girls' dances. The latter mark in their dance the place where the Elect will be confined, and whence she cannot move. The Elect is she whom the Spring is to consecrate, and who will give back to Spring the force that youth has taken from it.

The young girls dance about the Elect, a sort of glorification. Then comes the purification of the soil and the Evocation of the Ancestors. The Ancestors gather around the Elect, who begins the 'Dance of Consecration'. When she is on the point of falling exhausted, the Ancestors recognize it and glide toward her like rapacious monsters in order that she may not touch the ground; they pick her up and raise her toward heaven. The annual cycle of forces which are born again, and which fall again into the bosom of nature, is accomplished in its essential rhythms.

I am happy to have found in M. Nijinsky the ideal [choreographic] collaborator, and in M. Roerich, the creator of the decorative atmosphere for this work of faith.

'The Times', 12 July 1913, unsigned but by H. Colles, in 'Dossier de Presse', pp. 63–4

... The first performance of Stravinsky's *Le Sacre du Printemps* evoked something like a hostile demonstration from a section of the audience; the third and last performance was received with scarcely a sign of opposition, though doubtless a good deal of the applause was sympathetically intended for Mlle. Piltz, who bravely finished a terribly exacting dance in spite of an unfortunate accident. The fact remains that London audiences have settled down calmly to a new development of the ballet after a comparatively short acquaintance with it ...

A great deal of M. Stravinsky's work sounds unintelligible to its hearers for the reason that, up to the present, the music of a ballet has been dissociated from the dancing. This is caused by the fact that several of the earlier ballets (for example, *Les Sylphides*, *Carnival*, and *Le Spectre de la Rose*) have had their choreography fitted to music originally written for another purpose and well known to us in its original form. *L'Oiseau de Feu* and *Petrouchka* were the first heralds of a new order of things ...

... In *Le Sacre du Printemps*, on the other hand, the functions of the composer and the producer are so balanced that it is possible to see every movement on the stage and at the same time to hear every note of the music. But the fusion goes deeper than this. The combination of the two elements of music and dancing does actually produce a new compound result, expressible in terms of rhythm –

much as the combination of oxygen and hydrogen produces a totally different compound, water. Not only does M. Roerich's beautiful scenery also form an important part of the whole, but even the colours of the dresses are to some extent reflected in the orchestration – as, for instance, in the first scene, when a group of maidens in vivid scarlet huddles together to the accompaniment of closely-written chords on the trumpets. Movements, too, are mirrored in an equally realistic way where, a little later on, the dancers thin out into a straggling line, while the orchestra dwindles to a trill on the flutes; then a little tune begins in the woodwind two octaves apart, and two groups of three people detach themselves from either end of the line to begin a little dance that exactly suits the music. The same thing is seen equally clearly in the dance of the Chosen Maiden in the second scene, though as this is a solo dance the effect is less striking and more obvious. As regards gesture, the convention employed seems to be a treble one. First we have purely ritual movements of a primitive kind, such as leaping on the earth and looking towards the sun; then imitative or realistic gestures, seen when all the dancers shiver with terror at the entry of the old seer; and lastly movements of a purely emotional value, neither ritual nor imitative, which can be seen at their clearest in the dance by Mlle. Piltz already alluded to. These curious jerks of the body and sideways movements of the head are the modern descendants of the old-fashioned pirouette and *entre-chat*; and their artistic value seems to be about the same.

What is really of chief interest in the dancing is the employment of rhythmical counterpoint in the choral movements. There are many instances, from the curious mouse-like shufflings of the old woman against the rapid steps of the men in the first scene to the intricate rhythms of the joyful dance of the maidens in the last. But the most remarkable of all is to be found at the close of the first scene, where figures in scarlet run wildly round the stage in a great circle, while the shifting masses within are ceaselessly splitting up into tiny groups revolving on eccentric axes . . .

. . . Taking the music harmonically as a whole, it is evidently more intentionally bizarre than sincere . . . Realising to the full the vital importance of rhythm in this case, M. Stravinsky has let the actual sound of his music look after itself. We know from the researches of Dr C. S. Myers in Polynesia that savages perform ceremonial dances to the accompaniment of tom-toms, and that in them they employ rhythms so subtle as to be indistinguishable to Western ears. If M. Stravinsky had wished to be really primitive, he would have been wise to abandon his full orchestra and to score his ballet for nothing but drums.

Jacques Rivière, 'Le sacre du printemps', 'Nouvelle Revue Française',
November 1913. In 'Dossier de Presse', p. 44. Trans. Richard Buckle in
'Nijinsky', pp. 297–8

The only way to rediscover the source of all variety was first to pull the whole thing apart and then start by considering the emotions of the individual. This is what Nijinsky has done. Taking each group separately . . . he studied its cellular formation and recorded its instincts at the very moment of their birth; he became the observer and historian of its slightest impulse. The dancing of each group consists of movements hatched in isolation from the other groups, like those spontaneous fires that break out in haystacks. The absolute asymmetry which reigns throughout 'Le Sacre' is the very essence of the work . . . There is no lack of composition; on the contrary, there is the subtlest composition imaginable in the encounters, the challenges, the frays and the conflicts of these strange battalions. But composition does not take precedence over detail, does not condition it: it makes the best use it can of diverse elements. The impression of unity which we never cease for a moment to enjoy is like the sensation of watching the inhabitants of a given state moving about, passing, accosting and parting from each other, each intent on his own business, taking his neighbours for granted and putting them out of mind . . .

'Dancing for Diaghilev: The Memoirs of Lydia Sokolova', ed. Richard
Buckle, London, 1960, p. 38

In appearance Nijinsky was himself like a faun – a wild creature who had been trapped by society and was always ill at ease. When addressed, he turned his head furtively, looking as if he might suddenly butt you in the stomach. He moved on the balls of his feet, and his nervous energy found an outlet in fidgeting: when he sat down he twisted his fingers or played with his shoes. He hardly spoke to anyone, and seemed to exist on a different plane. Before dancing he was even more withdrawn, like a bewitched soul. I used to watch him practising his wonderful jumps in the first position, flickering his hands; I had never seen anyone like him before.

Lydia Sokolova in 'Dancing for Diaghilev', pp. 42–3

When I arrived in Monte Carlo the first of the two scenes in *Sacre* had already been arranged, and the English girls were merely fitted into the finale of that scene. This was complete chaos. We had to run about more or less *ad lib*, and stamp to various rhythms. We were really allotted no definite place on the stage, and the curtain came down on a stampede of humanity.

Marie Rambert had been especially engaged by Diaghilev to assist with the production of this ballet ... In previous ballets we had always been able to dance to a melody: in *Sacre* we had to dance to counts far more complicated than in *Faune*. I think this was easier for me than for some of the other dancers, because my musical studies had been quite advanced. Some of the girls used to be running around with little bits of paper in their hands, in a panic, quarrelling with each other about whose count was right and whose wrong.

In the first scene I remember a group of Ancients with long beards and hair, who stood huddled together, shaking and trembling as if they were dying with fear. The second scene, with the sacrifice of the Chosen Virgin, began with all the female dancers standing in a large circle facing outward, the Chosen One among them. We all had our toes pointing inwards, the right elbow resting on the left fist, and the right fist supporting the head which was leant sideways. As the ring began to move round, at certain counts the whole group would rise on tip-toe, dropping their right hands to their sides and jerking their heads to the left. When one circuit of the stage had been completed, every other girl would leap out of the ring, then back again.

The dance Nijinsky arranged for Piltz in the principal role was nothing like as strenuous, either mentally or physically, as the one I danced in the later Massine version, but it was effective all the same. Her dance was divided into sections, and knowing how difficult the phrasing is, I can see how much easier this was for her. Having the sequence of her movements interrupted by passages of ensemble dancing, she could simply begin every time with a new series of counts. (I only had two short breaks, when some steps to which I used to count five were echoed by the *corps de ballet*.) At the end of her dance, Piltz was lifted, lying full-length, onto the shoulders of the tallest men in the company; then as the music crashed to a close, they raised her to the full height of their upstretched arms and ran with her off the stage. This was a very impressive scene.

Lydia Sokolova in 'Dancing for Diaghilev', pp. 162–3

Without doubt the most terrifying experience of my life in the theatre was the first orchestra rehearsal of *Le Sacre* [1920 revival]. Igor Stravinsky, wearing an expression which would have frightened a hundred Chosen Virgins, pranced up and down the centre aisle of the [Théâtre des] Champs-Elysées, while Ansermet practised difficult passages of music with the orchestra. The cruel thing for me was that I had to wait about for the whole of the first act, with all the repetitions and corrections which were necessary. I became so scared that I nearly ran away. When the second scene began and my turn came to take the stage with the *corps de ballet*, I was so stunned that I couldn't hear the music, but the girls pulled me through the *ensemble* dances. When the other dancers retreated to the back of the stage and left me alone I thought I was going to faint. I stared at Ansermet: then I saw him make a sign of encouragement before he gave me the upbeat to begin. I danced; and I met the orchestra precisely at the two places where I should, and we finished together. After that I knew I never had anything to fear from the orchestra when Ansermet was conducting. He understood the dance, and could tell exactly how I was progressing as it mounted to its final climax . . . When the time came to try on the old costumes for *Le Sacre*, which were to be used again, I was given one of the red ones from the first act. I found I could not get through my dance in this thick flannel dress and stuffy wig. A new tunic was therefore made in white silk, so that I should have the least possible weight on my body . . . To prevent it falling across my face and obscuring my vision when I performed the big, hammering steps round the stage, flinging my body from side to side, the top part of my hair by my neck was stitched together by criss-cross tacking stitches with double thread.

Siegfried Sassoon, 'Concert-Interpretation (Le Sacre du Printemps)',
1921 (extracts)

The Audience pricks an intellectual Ear . . .
Stravinsky . . . Quite the Concert of the Year!
*   *   *
Forgetting now that none-so-distant date
When they (or folk facsimilar in state
Of mind) first heard with hisses – hoots – guffaws
This abstract Symphony; (they booed because
Stravinsky jumped their Wagner palisade
With modes that seemed cacophonous and queer;)
Forgetting now the hullabaloo they made,
The Audience pricks an intellectual Ear.
*   *   *
But savagery pervades Me; I am frantic
With corybantic rupturing of laws.
Come, dance, and seize this clamorous chance to function
Creatively, – abandoning compunction

In anti-social rhapsodic applause!
Lynch the conductor! Jugulate the drums!
Butcher the brass! Ensanguinate the strings!
Throttle the flutes! ... Stravinsky's April comes
With pitiless pomp and pain of sacred springs ...
Incendiarize the Hall with resinous fires
Of sacrificial fiddles scorched and snapping! ...

Eugene Goossens, 'Overture and Beginners, London, 1951', p. 162

I asked Mr Bernard Shaw, who had been indefatigable in attendance at performances and discussions of modern music all the week, to give the *Observer* readers the view of our oldest music critic, and he replied regarding this particular work: 'Mind, I am not to be understood as condemning it, but if it had been by Rossini, people would have said that there was too much "rumtum" in it.'

Ernest Newman, 'The Sunday Times', 3 July 1921, in 'Dossier de Presse', p. 75

... The next time they proclaim that they, by special revelation from on high, have discovered *the* great man and *the* work of the century, some joker will be sure to smile and murmur 'Le Sacre du Printemps!'

Cecil Gray 'A Survey of Contemporary Music', London, 1927

... in the same way that an hypnotic concentration on purely harmonic interest involves a corresponding loss of harmonic strength – so Stravinsky's obsession with rhythm in the *Sacre* has led, not only to the impoverishment of both harmony and melody, but to the loss of the very quality to which he sacrificed the other two – rhythmic vitality. The *Sacre du Printemps*, so far from being the triumphant apotheosis of rhythm, the act of restoration to its rightful supremacy of the most important and essential element of musical expression, is the very negation and denial of rhythm. In sacrificing everything to it, Stravinsky has, with admirable poetic justice, lost it, along with its companions, as well. Rhythm has here degenerated into metre.
  ... even those sections of the *Sacre* which give the impression of complexity, such as the final dance of the Elect, in which every musical interest is sacrificed

to rhythmical purposes, are very primitive in construction. The time-signature changes constantly from bar to bar, but the music itself does not; it is only the eye and not the ear which perceives the changes. There is nothing there but the incessant reiteration of the same insignificant metrical phrase in slightly varying quantities – regular measures with irregularly recurring *cæsure*. Strip the music of the bar-lines and time-signatures, which are only a loincloth concealing its shameful nudity, and it will at once be seen that there is no rhythm at all. Rhythm implies life, some kind of movement or progression at least, but this music stands quite still, in a quite frightening immobility. It is like a top or gyroscope turning ceaselessly and ineffectually on itself, without moving an inch in any direction, until, in the last bars of the work, it suddenly falls over on its side with a lurch, and stops dead.

It is depressing to reflect that such things should be accepted as remarkable rhythmical achievements by a nation which, perhaps more than any other, can justly pride itself on having produced supreme masters of rhythm, both musical and verbal. There is more rhythm in a song of Dowland or in a madrigal of Weelkes or Wilbye than in all the works of Stravinsky put together.

Pierre Boulez, 'Stocktakings from an Apprenticeship', Oxford, 1991, p. 107

All things considered, I conclude that this work has, in spite of and thanks to its defects, as great a value in the evolution of music as, for example, *Pierrot Lunaire*. For, while one can perpetuate nothing of the tonal method of the *Rite*, which is a mere survival (as is that of *The Wedding*), the rhythmic technique, by contrast, still remains practically unexplored, at least as regards its internal consequences; no one will dispute that certain more or less mechanized procedures have been plated on to contemporary language in the form of rhythmic colouring, just as a superficial tonal colouring has been achieved with a few intervals of an anarchic tendency. It is worth saying that few works in musical history can pride themselves on not having exhausted their potential for innovation forty years on. Here, the innovation is on a single plane, that of rhythm; but even with this limitation, it represents a degree of invention and a quality of discovery that are deeply to be envied.

In the conclusions I have drawn from my different analyses, I may perhaps be accused of exaggerating the arithmetical relationships and paying too little attention to the unconscious. Need I repeat that I make no claim to having discovered a creative process, but only to having understood the result, the arithmetical relationships being the only ones that are tangible? If I have succeeded in noting all these structural features, it is because they are there, and it therefore makes no difference to me whether they were put there consciously or unconsciously, or with what degree of acuity of conceptual intelligence, or even with what interactions between perspiration and inspiration. To establish such a genesis for the *Rite* would be of great speculative interest, but would miss the purely musical goal that I wanted to set myself.

Isaiah Berlin, 1964, quoted in 'The Daily Telegraph', 3 August 1996

One day Stravinsky rang me up and asked me if I would book some seats for *The Marriage of Figaro* at Covent Garden. I had never heard of him going to concerts or listening to any music by people other than himself. But orders is orders, I thought, so I booked the seats. It emerged that Stravinsky had deliberately chosen the night of the 50th anniversary of *The Rite of Spring* when Pierre Monteux was to conduct a special performance at the Albert Hall.

'Monteux's a terrible conductor; he will ruin my music,' explained Stravinsky. 'Nothing in the world could persuade me to go and hear my music being murdered by this frightful butcher.' So he was told, 'Look, Maestro, if you remain in the Savoy, then I think you might just get away with it. But if you are seen somewhere else...'

Eventually, Stravinsky agreed to remain at Covent Garden for only one act. He calculated metronomically how long Monteux's performance would take, and arranged to have a taxi waiting to take him to the Albert Hall, where he could go out and take a bow. But when we began leaving the Opera House after an hour, an usherette came towards us and said 'You can't leave now. This is not an interval. It's only a dim-out.' Stravinsky turned red, said in a voice of absolute thunder 'we *all* have diarrhoea'. The usherette more or less fell over backwards, and off he went in his taxi. Next day there were photographs of Monteux embracing Stravinsky, Stravinsky embracing Monteux, and not a dry eye in the hall.

Lawrence Morton, 'Tempo' 128, March 1979, pp. 10–12

... the poet who concerns us here is the promising young Gorodetsky of 1907. His *Yar* is a book of some 60 poems. Two of them, 'Spring (The Cloister)' and 'Song of the Dew (The Flagellants)', took Stravinsky's fancy and he set them to music – the first late in the year, the second early in 1908. One can assume that Stravinsky read the book complete before he selected two of the poems for song-texts. If so, he certainly read, on pages 23–24, a poem entitled 'Yarila'.

This title is the name of one of the principal gods of Slavonic pre-Christian mythology, a name that has been associated etymologically with Eros and also with *yarovoi*, the spring corn-planting. Because celebrations in his honour were often orgiastic, he has also been linked with Dionysus. But in his principal mythological role he was the god of spring and fecundity. It is as such, as the new-born god of spring, that Gorodetsky deals with him in 'Yarila'.

First to sharpen the ax-flint they bent,
On the green they had gathered, unpent,
They had gathered beneath the green tent,
There where whitens a pale tree-trunk, naked,
There where whitens a pale linden trunk,
By the linden tree, by the young linden,
The linden trunk
White and naked.

At the fore, shaggy, lean, hoar of head,
Moves the wizard, as old as his runes;
He has lived over two thousand moons,
And the ax he inhumed.
On the far lakes he loomed
Long ago.
It is his: the first blow
At the trunk.

And two priestesses in their tenth Spring
To the old one they bring.
In their eyes
Terror lies.
Like the trunk their young bodies are bright.
Their wan white
Has she only, the tender young linden.

One he took, one he led,
To the trunk roughly wed,
A white bride.
And the ax rose and hissed –
And a voice was upraised
And then died.
Thus the first blow was dealt to the trunk.

Others followed him, others upraised
The age-old bloody ax,
That keen, flint-bladed ax:
The flesh once,
The tree twice
Fiercely cleaving.

And the trunk reddened fast,
And it took on a face.
Lo, – this notch is a nose,
This – an eye.
The flesh once,
The trunk twice –
Till all red was the rise
And the green crimsoned deep.
On the sod
In the red stains there lies
A new god.[1]

In these lines, unmistakably, lie the essential elements of Stravinsky's dream of *Le Sacre du Printemps*: a pagan rite, the sage elders, the sacrifice of a young girl to propitiate the god of spring. The likeness is too close to be coincidental. This conjecture has been reinforced by the reaction of both Russian and English readers to whom the poem has been shown. Recognition occurs inevitably no later than the third or fourth stanza, and always with an exclamatory, 'It's *Le Sacre*!'.

Without delving into the psychology of dreams, visions, and memory, one can still conclude that 'Yarila', once read by Stravinsky in 1907, was never given another thought. The subject matter held no interest for him. Discarded, it nevertheless dropped into that 'deep well of the unconscious' where it remained for three years, ready to be summoned into consciousness when some external influence would stimulate its release. 'Dreams are my psychological digestive system', Stravinsky wrote; and the 'Yarila'-*Sacre* complex is a nice example of how raw material is stored, combined with other elements, and finally put to use by the creative faculty. Just as Purchas's 'goodly Damosels skilfull in Songs and Instruments of Musicke and Dancing' became in Coleridge's dream 'A damsel with a dulcimer', so Gorodetsky's white bride, wed to the linden in a bloody rite, became in Stravinsky's dream the sacrificial virgin of *Le Sacre*'s death-dance.

7

Stravinsky's collaborators

Nowhere is Stravinsky's later disenchantment with the original production of the *Rite* more emphatic than in his venomous demolition of Nijinsky. The *Rite* has a special place in Nijinsky's small output as a choreographer:[1] it was the only ballet he created in which he himself did not appear as dancer, and the only one in which he worked closely with a composer, in this case one whose language and culture he shared.[2] Nonetheless Nijinsky's contribution to the *Rite* was unusual, in that he had played no part in the ballet's conception. In this the *Rite* contrasts with *Jeux*, the other ballet created by Nijinsky in 1913, in which he had a considerable hand in the story and perhaps also the detailed scenario.[3] Nijinsky was, of course, familiar with Stravinsky's most recent music, having created the role of Petrushka in the 1911 season, a legendary performance and one greatly admired by Stravinsky, who referred to Nijinsky's 'unsurpassed rendering...'[4]

Despite this pedigree, Stravinsky – writing in his autobiography some twenty years after the event – claims he had misgivings from the outset.

The poor boy knew nothing of music. He could neither read it nor play any instrument, and his reactions to music were expressed in banal phrases or the repetition of what he had heard others say... My apprehensions can readily be understood... Nijinsky began by demanding such a fantastic number of rehearsals that it was physically impossible to give them to him. It will not be difficult to understand why he wanted so many, when I say that in trying to explain to him the construction of my work in general outline and in detail I discovered that I should achieve nothing until I had taught him the very rudiments of music... He had the greatest difficulty in remembering any of this. ...It was exasperating and we advanced at a snail's pace. It was all the more trying because Nijinsky complicated and encumbered his dances beyond all reason, thus creating difficulties for the dancers that were sometimes impossible to overcome. This was due as much to his lack of experience as to the complexity of the task with which he was unfamiliar... [He] became presumptuous, capricious, and unmanageable. The natural result was a series of painful incidents which seriously complicated matters.[5]

Stravinsky's later recollections repeat all this. The dance 'often had nothing to do with the music. "I will count to forty while you play", Nijinsky would say to me, "and we will see where we come out." He could not understand that though we might at some point come out together, this did not necessarily mean we had been together on the way'.[6]

The nub of this damning account – leaving aside the question of Nijinsky's musical competence – is Stravinsky's allegation that the choreography was too complicated. It is certainly true that the choreography was an ambitious attempt to match the music rhythm by rhythm. As Marie Rambert recalled – 'Nijinsky... wanted very much to translate every note of the music...' In her view he was right. 'Because the music was so powerful, and its rhythmic impact so tremendous... when it was all done by a company of magnificent dancers as they were, that practically doubled the impact of what Stravinsky had written.'[7] Rambert had been engaged by Diaghilev to assist Nijinsky. She was a pupil of Emile Jacques-Dalcroze, inventor of eurythmics, and as such she could help Nijinsky with teaching the complex rhythms of the *Rite* to the dancers. Like Stravinsky, Rambert kept an annotated version of the four-hand score in which she recorded Nijinsky's verbal instructions.[8] These became the basis for the reconstruction of the original choreography in a production of the *Rite* by the Joffrey Ballet in 1987.[9]

A specific complaint of Stravinsky's was that Nijinsky had slowed the tempo of the music in order to fit with his over-complicated steps. 'Many choreographers have that fault, but I have never known any who erred in that respect to the same degree as Nijinsky.'[10] And in his later account Stravinsky complained that, with the dancers following not the music but Nijinsky's counting, 'in fast-tempo movements, neither he nor they could keep pace with the music'.[11] Again Marie Rambert's recollections provide support. A page of her notes for the opening of 'Ritual of Abduction' appears to show that Nijinsky had altered or (more likely) misjudged the tempo since there were too many steps to be danced in the time available[12] – hence the flaming row which Rambert describes between Stravinsky and Nijinsky.[13]

Then into this confusion and bad blood came the startling claim that much of the planning of the choreography – at least in outline – was Stravinsky's.

This about-turn arose from the discovery of a four-hand score with annotations in Stravinsky's handwriting. These 'choreographic notes' were published as part of an appendix to the *Sketches* in 1969. In a short introductory essay, Stravinsky asserted that his choreographic notes were not a record of what Nijinsky had devised, but that on the contrary they represented '*my* [my emphasis] markings for Nijinsky ... The score records most of *my* [my emphasis] original plan of choreographic movement...'[14] In one respect at least, Stravinsky must be wrong. These notes cannot be a document that Stravinsky gave to Nijinsky, since they were made on a *printed* score of the four-hand version which was not published until a few days before the première, far too late to be of use to Nijinsky. At best they must be a copy of such notes; more probably they are a note of the salient points of the choreography which Stravinsky thought it worthwhile to record.[15]

Nonetheless, Stravinsky's four-hand score shows the closeness of the Stravinsky–Nijinsky collaboration. Remarkably, the steps of the dancers were intended to add a further layer of rhythm in counterpoint to the rhythms of the music. At the opening of 'The Ritual of Abduction', for example, Stravinsky's notes reveal that the dancers were to emphasise the first beats of bars 1, 2, 3 and 7 – bars 2 and 3 being marked by 'jumps', in contrast to the accents in the orchestra which at this point are all off the beat. Much the same occurs in the famous opening bars of 'The Augurs of Spring' where choreographic accents on the first beats of bars 3, 5, 6, 7 and 8 appear to trigger the syncopations in the orchestra – which, as we have seen, really are 'syncopations' given the firmly established 2/4 metre which the dancers confirm. In 'Spring Rounds' the rhythm of the music is overlaid by three layers of danced rhythms, each with its own rhythm. In Stravinsky's piano duet score these are notated on an additional single-line stave drawn in by hand, rather as if the rhythms belonged to additional percussion instruments.[16]

The clear implication from all this is that, if there were ructions and difficulties at rehearsals, they were not so much the product of Nijinsky's

artistic ambition or inexperience as the combination of it with the
extraordinary demands made on all concerned by Stravinsky himself. If
the choreography was over-complicated and impractical it was at least as
much the composer's fault as Nijinsky's. Stravinsky had the decency, in
1969, to withdraw his earlier accounts – 'this account of the choreography supersedes all others, including those testaments of my own faulty
memory now permanently on exhibit elsewhere'. But is it credible that
in writing his autobiography (in 1935) Stravinsky's memory should have
been so 'faulty' over events which had taken place only twenty years
earlier?

There is another explanation for Stravinsky's unhappy memory of
events at this time, and for the contortions we see in his changing
accounts. The composer's work on the *Rite* was soured by Diaghilev's
jealousy of his having originated the idea with Roerich independently of
the impresario, upon whom Stravinsky had until then been virtually
dependent. Diaghilev had, in losing patience with the over-weening
Fokine and substituting Nijinsky (whom he thought would be more
malleable as a protégé) foisted an inexperienced and demanding collaborator on Stravinsky, and had effectively asserted his own right to have a
say in the production of this ballet in the way that he had contributed to
Firebird and *Petrushka*. Stravinsky's unrecorded but likely unease (to put
it no stronger) at Diaghilev's homosexuality is clearly behind some of the
barbed attacks which were later focused on Nijinsky. Nijinsky was the
vehicle through which Diaghilev exercised his power over Stravinsky,
and it is a measure of the composer's recognition of the quality
of Nijinsky's work that their collaboration worked as well as it did.
Diaghilev, by contrast, was barely ever mentioned by Stravinsky in
his writings and interviews. We can speculate that the foul response
Diaghilev had made to Stravinsky's news of his project with Roerich had
been a wholly inaccurate and (to Stravinsky) hurtful assertion about the
nature of their relationship: after this unhappy beginning, Stravinsky
found himself caught up in the intrigues of a covert gay relationship
between Diaghilev and Nijinsky so it is hardly surprising that the
enormous influence of Diaghilev was never duly acknowledged in
Stravinsky's later accounts.[17]

This glimpse of Stravinsky having a say in all aspects of the new ballet
is in marked contrast with his earlier collaborations with Fokine (*Fire-*

bird) and Benois (*Petrushka*), where it was the music which had to submit to the demands of the choreographer and of the scenario – with Stravinsky working as a somewhat junior partner. It shows also the profound interest Stravinsky took in the balletic realisation of his score, and his completely practical approach to solving its unprecedented difficulties.

Stravinsky would hardly have pursued so ambitious a plan if he had harboured doubts about Nijinsky's competence. Indeed all the evidence suggests that at the time of the première Stravinsky held Nijinsky in high regard. In the early stages of rehearsals he wrote to N. F. Findeyzen – 'Nijinsky directs [the *Rite*] with passionate zeal and with complete self-effacement.'[18] Findeyzen was the editor of a magazine, Stravinsky's remark being intended therefore for public consumption. But the opinions he expressed in private letters were equally warm. Later – significantly after the disastrous première of the *Rite*, the only performance of the original production which Stravinsky attended – he wrote to Maximilien Steinberg, a fellow-pupil of Rimsky-Korsakov – 'Nijinsky's choreography was incomparable; with the exception of a few places, everything was as I wanted it.'[19] Stravinsky later wrote to Benois after Nijinsky's marriage (in Buenos Aires, 10 September 1913), in the realisation that this would irrevocably remove Nijinsky from Diaghilev's circle, thus effectively ending his work as a choreographer – 'For me the hope of seeing something valuable in choreography has been removed for a long time to come.'[20]

Although the memoirs of members of Diaghilev's company make clear how difficult Nijinsky could be to work with, all in various ways express admiration for his work. His sister, Bronislava Nijinska, addresses Stravinsky's criticisms in her memoirs. Originally cast as the Chosen One (she was forced to give up the role on the discovery of her pregnancy, in March 1913), she recalls early rehearsals for the 'Sacrificial Dance' which took place before the main rehearsals with the company. 'In ... this part of the choreography of *Sacre*, Vaslav did not "graphically" render each musical note by a physical movement, nor did he have recourse to counting the beats aloud...' Nijinska attributes the counting (derided by Stravinsky) to the malign influence of the Dalcroze eurythmics made fashionable by Isadora Duncan which Diaghilev had foisted on the company.[21]

Moreover her brother was exasperated by Stravinsky's patronising attitude. 'I have great respect for him as a musician, and we have been friends for years, but so much time is wasted as Stravinsky thinks he is the only one who knows anything about music. In working with me he explains the value of the black notes, the white notes, of quavers and semiquavers, as though I had never studied music at all... I wish he would talk more about *his* music for *Sacre*, and not give a lecture on the beginning [*sic*] theory of music.'[22]

Equally, Nijinsky was in the habit of working very slowly, as he had on *L'Après-midi d'un faune*, for which a legendary number of rehearsals had been required. According to Rambert 'words did not come easily to him, which is why the rehearsing of his ballet always took so long. But he demonstrated the movement so perfectly that he left no doubt as to the way it had to be done.'[23] His approach was the opposite of Fokine, who encouraged dancers to develop their own ideas on characterisation. With Nijinsky everything was meticulously planned and under his control. He once berated a dancer, saying that the expression of her personal feelings was of no concern.[24]

The first step in Stravinsky's disavowal of his collaborator came in the run-up to the revival of the *Rite* in Paris in 1920. Although Roerich's sets and costumes were retained,[25] the new choreography by Massine[26] gave Stravinsky the opportunity to make comparisons with the 1913 production. Though still complimentary (he describes Nijinsky's choreography as having had 'great plastic beauty') he disparages the old version with a ruthless disregard for the truth. 'Massine', he says, 'underlines the music better than a note-by-note transfer, which was the error of the old choreography...' Perversely, Stravinsky describes the 1913 production as 'subjected to the tyranny of the bar...',[27] quite the opposite of what the annotations in the four-hand score reveal.[28] But as we have seen, there was more to Stravinsky's rewriting of history than just 'talking up' the new production. More importantly, Stravinsky emphasises the integrity of the music, which 'exists as a piece of music first and last';[29] and '... far from being descriptive, the music was an "objective construction"'.[30] As Craft puts it, 'The real preference expressed here is not for the work of Nijinsky or Massine, but for concert rather than staged performance.'[31] Remember that while the *ballet* had been 'abused',

Monteux's concert performance in 1914 had been a triumph. This was not the first Stravinsky stage work to benefit in this way. Monteux had written to Stravinsky *à propos Petrushka*: 'How this music gains by being played in concert, since all the details are heard,' a remark Stravinsky underlined in red pencil.[32] Much later – in *Expositions and Developments* – Stravinsky recalled the circumstances – 'Monteux was doubtful about programming *Le Sacre*, in view of the original scandal, but he had enjoyed a great success with a performance of *Petroushka* meanwhile, and he was proud of his prestige among avant-garde musicians; I argued, too, that *Le Sacre* was more symphonic, more of a concert piece, than *Petroushka*.'[33]

In keeping (perhaps) with this, Stravinsky's view of the *Rite* in 1920 was entirely abstract. '[Massine] and I have suppressed all anecdotal detail, symbolism, etc. [that might] obscure this work of purely musical construction... There is no story at all and no point in looking for one ... and no subject. The choreography is constructed freely on the music.'[34] This is certainly out of step with the recollection of Massine, who remembered his version as based on 'the simple movements of the Russian peasants' "round dances"'.[35]

Why then did Stravinsky's view of 1913, which in 1920 was still polite if wilfully inaccurate, evolve in the next few years into the appallingly derogatory account of the autobiography of 1935, to which must be added the account in *Expositions and Developments* with its gratuitously offensive descriptions of the dance and the dancers – 'knock-kneed and long-braided Lolitas'.[36] Why this *animus* towards Nijinsky, who could of course have no possibility of defending himself?[37]

What lies behind this shabby story is the evolution of Stravinsky's own attitude to the *Rite*. The first step is marked by the article in *Montjoie!* which appeared under Stravinsky's name on the morning of the première and which continued to irritate Stravinsky for the rest of his life. The full text is printed in Chapter 6 since, if it is genuine, it is a document of paramount interest. The article is disowned in Stravinsky's autobiography.

Among the most assiduous onlookers at the rehearsals had been a certain Ricciotto Canuedo [*sic*], a charming man, devoted to everything advanced and up to date. He was at that time publishing a review called *Montjoie!*

When he asked me for an interview, I very willingly granted it. Unfortunately it appeared in the form of a pronouncement on *Le Sacre*, at once grandiloquent and naive, and, to my great astonishment, signed with my name. I could not recognise myself, and was much disturbed by this distortion of my language and even of my ideas, especially as the pronouncement was generally regarded as authentic, and the scandal over *Le Sacre* had noticeably increased the sale of the review.[38]

The article appeared on the morning of the première, 29 May. Within a few days (though ill with typhus) Stravinsky repudiated it in a letter which Canudo published in *Montjoie!* on 5 June. Canudo, not surprisingly, reacted with dismay – 'Since *Montjoie!* sought to give you support and encouragement, surely I have the right not to understand your animosity.'[39] Indeed, perhaps the most extraordinary aspect of Stravinsky's vehement public denial is that it risked making enemies of a sympathetic journalist and magazine. Incidentally, the extent to which Stravinsky was aware of the need to cultivate friendly critics is shown by his assiduous wooing of Florent Schmitt, who reviewed the *Rite* enthusiastically in *La France* on 4 June 1913, and who renamed his house at Auteuil, the venue for a private pre-première audition of the *Rite* in November 1912, *Villa Oiseau de feu*.[40]

However, in August, a letter written by Stravinsky to V. V. Derzhanovsky, editor of the Russian journal *Muzyka*, makes it clear that Stravinsky was indeed the author of the *Montjoie!* article. The purpose of the letter was to complain of an unauthorised translation of the article which was published in *Muzyka* on 16 August 1913.[41] Stravinsky even went to the trouble of revising the Russian translation in the hope that this would be published in *Muzyka* (it never was). Stravinsky's annotated copy of the offending Russian version reveals that his changes are largely cosmetic.[42]

A comparison with the original article shows that Stravinsky's objections were to the revision's language rather than the article's substance. Many of the ideas are characteristic of Stravinsky, and indeed could only have come from him. 'In the Prelude [the "Introduction" to Part I] I have brought forward the wind instruments which have a drier tone, which are more precise, less endowed with facile expression, and on this account more suitable for my purpose.'[43] Indeed so: this passage highlights one of the *Rite*'s characteristics most prophetic of Stravinsky's later music. Doubtless, however, Stravinsky found embarrassing the interpretation of the same music – 'In the Prelude, before the curtain rises, I have confided to my orchestra the great fear which weighs on every sensitive soul ... etc. etc.'

In short, either Stravinsky did write the article, and immediately regretted it; or (just possibly) he was the victim of a ghost-writer on whom he kept (being busy with rehearsals for the première) an insufficiently close eye.[44]

Nikolai Roerich, Stravinsky's other principal collaborator, escapes relatively lightly in later memoirs. 'I still have a good opinion of Roerich's *Le Sacre*. He had designed a backdrop of steppes and sky, the *Hic Sunt Leones* country of old mapmakers' imaginations. The row of twelve blonde, square-shouldered girls against this landscape made a very striking tableau.'[45]

Nonetheless Stravinsky's later accounts give no idea of Roerich's seminal role.[46] As Craft puts it – 'Roerich was the catalyst of the subject, an incomparably more effective function than that of set and costume designer by which he is remembered.'[47] In particular the valuable and voluminous research by Richard Taruskin has revealed the extent to which the *Rite* was embedded in folk ritual. Quite apart from the set designs and the costumes – the latter modelled, as we have seen, on authentic examples in the collection of Princess Tenisheva – Roerich was responsible for every detail in the scenario. Stravinsky's only contribution was the initial impulse (the dream or vision) together with the division of the work into two halves, day and night. The pursuit of authenticity extended even to the content of the music, and Taruskin has shown that it was very probably Roerich who pointed Stravinsky towards appropriate folk melodies.

The other reason which Stravinsky later gave for approaching Roerich was that he knew that in his designs 'he would not overload'. This seems faint praise. Yet, in reality it seems a legitimate expression of what Stravinsky and Roerich were about, the search for authenticity instead of the 'made for export' Russianness he disliked in the sets and costumes for *Firebird*.[48] Moreover Stravinsky may well have felt that with Roerich he would not be subject to the sort of fussy interventions he had endured from Benois and Fokine during that ballet's preparation.

The extent of Roerich's influence on Nijinsky is recalled by his sister, Bronislava Nijinska. She quotes her brother as saying: 'Roerich is not only a great artist but also a philosopher and scholar... Now that I am working on *Sacre* Roerich's art inspires me as much as does Stravinsky's powerful music... Roerich has talked to me at length about his paintings in this series that he describes as the awakening of the spirit of primeval man. In *Sacre* I want to emulate this spirit of the prehistoric Slavs.'[49] Elsewhere Nijinska comments: 'Only Roerich supported Vaslav. He often came to the rehearsals and encouraged Vaslav, who would listen attentively. The only time Vaslav appeared relaxed during rehearsals was when he was with Roerich.'[50]

What of the musical fruits of the Roerich–Stravinsky collaboration? Their intention seems to have been nothing less than to create an entirely primitive, 'pre-artistic' music. Musically, there was one possible source which could be tapped, the traditional music of rural Russia, still surviving though in decline. The stroke of genius was the decision not to use these folk melodies as quotations, nor as splashes of 'local colour' (as in *Petrushka*), but buried deep within the musical fabric. To do this Stravinsky created a sort of imaginary folk music out of real folk music, transforming the originals almost beyond recognition. Naturally when Stravinsky later denied the importance of the Roerich–Stravinsky libretto, he had also to cover his tracks as regards folk music.[51]

There is an alternative explanation, however, which may acquit Stravinsky of deception. For one thing, if Stravinsky was trying to mislead it is odd that he should have told Schæffner the source of the bassoon melody. Some day someone was bound to look it up: someone did, albeit nearly fifty years after Schæffner. According to Craft, Stravinsky was genuinely indifferent to the subject in later life – 'the question of originality, of fabrication or ethnological authenticity, is of no interest to him'.[52] This is straightforward revisionism, not to be taken at face value. To be a little cynical, Stravinsky had every reason to be reticent. When composing *Petrushka* he had adopted a commonplace street tune, 'Elle avait une jambe de bois' (two bars after fig. 13), which he had heard played under his window at Beaulieu-sur-Mer. By extraordinary ill luck, this turned out to be in copyright. The composer was one Emile Spencer, who died in 1921. By 1932 the publisher of Spencer's tune was receiving approximately a tenth share of Stravinsky's royalty earnings for *Petrushka*.[53]

Granted the immense importance of Roerich's contribution, there was a gulf in sensibility between him and Stravinsky. The common ground was Roerich's belief in 'the refined primitivism of our ancestors, for whom rhythm, the sacred symbol, and subtlety of movement were great and sacred concepts'.[54] Certainly, as we have seen, there is no shortage of intricacy and subtlety in Stravinsky's music. Yet from the very first bars Stravinsky sketched, the music has the 'strong and brutal manner' of Stravinsky's later description in *Comœdia Illustré*. There is no parallel in Roerich's art to the agitated, multi-layered, internally battling textures which characterise the score. Compare Stravinsky's interpretation of their joint scenario with the sublime vision and misty nostalgia of Roerich's paintings.[55]

As we have seen, Stravinsky's complete renunciation of the *Rite*'s true origins comes in 1920, when he stresses that the setting in prehistoric Russia was simply an apt way of expressing the music. The music, he emphasises, came first. There was, of course, no more truth in this than in the later excoriation of Nijinsky. This 1920 article is the most extreme attempt by Stravinsky to divorce the music from its original *raison d'être*. The signs are, however, that the process of denial had begun much earlier.

One reason, undoubtedly, was the devastating effect on Stravinsky of the scandal at the first performance. For us this may be hard to understand, with public hostility to the first appearance of masterpieces being a cliché of musical history. As Florent Schmitt wrote in his notice of the first performance – '... The genius of Igor Stravinsky could not have received more striking confirmation than in the incomprehension of the audience and its malicious hostility.'[56] It certainly does not seem to have perturbed Diaghilev.[57] But Stravinsky, we need to remember, was abnormally touchy about adverse criticism – and even of implied criticism: witness his ferocious reaction to Ansermet's request to make a small cut in *Jeu de cartes*, an episode which soured a valued friendship and professional association.[58] This was a man who, nearly seventy years after the event, could still recall every detail of a childhood humiliation – 'One evening at dinner my father ... asked me what new French word I had learned. I blushed, hesitated, blurted out *parqwa* (*pourquoi*), and then started to cry. Everyone laughed and made great fun of me ... I cannot forget ... and to forgive has no meaning now ...'[59] And fifty-five years after the première of the *Rite* Stravinsky inscribed the first autograph full score (of March 1913) – 'May whoever listens to this music never experience the mockery to which it was subjected and of which I was the witness...'[60]

But it was more than just the effect of criticism and controversy. Consider Stravinsky's very odd behaviour, after and even before the première. First there was his failure to attend any of Monteux's preliminary orchestral rehearsals. True, Stravinsky was busy with the reorchestration for Diaghilev of parts of Musorgsky's *Khovanshchina*, but the omission is extraordinary, and was obviously felt to be so by Monteux. Then, on 2 June Stravinsky seems not to have attended the second performance of the *Rite* [61] – he was unable to attend any of the performances that summer in Paris or London after contracting typhus as a result of eating oysters the following day, 3 June.[62] Then, despite the typhus, he busied himself with the public – and very dubious – denial of the *Montjoie!* article which had appeared on 29 May.

The final – and most telling – evidence as to Stravinsky's state of mind was the fate of the choreographic notes. These, it will be remembered, were made on a printed copy of the piano four-hand score, published on 21 May.[63] What reason could Stravinsky have had for making these notes if not as a record of the choreography and its relation to the rhythms of the music, to be used in some future production? Then, suddenly, on the day after the première, he gives them away.[64]

Is it possible in all this to disentangle the truth? To begin at the beginning: Stravinsky conceived (in a dream or vision) the subject for a ballet. The image of a maiden dancing in front of elders quickly developed into the idea of human sacrifice, and thence to a setting in remote prehistory. For this reason – and probably also because Stravinsky sensed the need for rigorous authenticity to guard against 'kitsch' – he approached Roerich. He was influenced by Roerich, who was artistically the more experienced of the two, and possibly by the work and ideals at Talashkino. He worked closely with Nijinsky, whom he admired, as he had with Roerich.[65] The première of 29 May 1913 came as a terrible shock, especially after three years (since the première of *Firebird*) in which Stravinsky had grown accustomed to being lionised. But the première also revealed a truth which Stravinsky had already suspected: the disunity between stage and music. Quite simply, the music, which had begun as the expression of the scenario, had outgrown it.[66] Perhaps a rift was inevitable, since in the year and a half since approaching Roerich and starting work on the music, Stravinsky had travelled so fast and so far: *Petrushka* had transformed him.

The mismatch cut three ways. As far as Roerich's contribution is concerned, few people seem to have noticed his designs, and those that did thought them old-fashioned – 'fusty romanticism' was Roger Fry's description.[67] Nijinsky's choreography, on the other hand, attracted serious and interested comment (Colles, Rivière). Indeed dance historians clearly regard Nijinsky as a choreographer of major importance. In the *Rite* Nijinsky seems to have understood the 'pitiless' quality of Stravinsky's music, moving the dancers in impersonal blocks, the reverse of the characterisation encouraged by Fokine with the crowd scenes in *Petrushka*.[68] Why then was it Nijinsky, not Roerich, whom Stravinsky attacked? Perhaps jealousy, with Nijinsky stealing some of his thunder; perhaps also a genuine feeling that the choreography had been misconceived, over-complicated (though, as we have seen, that was as much Stravinsky's fault as Nijinsky's). Most of all, I suspect, because if Stravinsky wished to detach the *Rite* from its original conception, the admired work of Nijinsky posed much more of a threat than that of Roerich.

At once Stravinsky sought to loosen the *Rite* from its origins, the first step being to deny his authorship of the *Montjoie!* article, with its heavily symbolic interpretation of the music and the dance. Then the triumphant concert performance of April 1914 showed him the way forward. When the *Rite* resurfaced in 1920 he told an outright lie, to the effect that the original scenario had simply been an interpretation of the music, not the other way round. Having embarked on this course, Stravinsky sought to shift the blame for the 1913 debacle by choosing a scapegoat (Nijinsky). The story is not a pretty one. Nonetheless, in Stravinsky's defence, we should not confuse the *origins* of a work of art – what it set out to be – with what it is, or later becomes. Artistically Stravinsky's behaviour is understandable, even if on a human level it seems deplorable.

8

The Rite *recorded*

The year of the *Rite*'s first performance (1913) is memorable for another milestone in the history of music, the first complete recording of a major symphonic work – Beethoven's Fifth Symphony, with the Berlin Philharmonic Orchestra conducted by Artur Nikisch. Thus by chance the *Rite* in performance matured, and (as we shall see) grew middle-aged, exactly in tandem with the emerging record industry, reinvigorated by each technical development – the invention of the microphone, tape editing, the long playing record, stereo, the compact disc. Stravinsky at first backed the wrong horse, preferring the mechanical piano or pianola to the gramophone. Stravinsky's interest in the pianola may well have originated in his mistrust of rehearsal pianists: he suggested to Diaghilev that he should use a pianola for rehearsals of the *Rite*.[1] Then, after the introduction of the microphone, when it became possible to record orchestras on location and with much greater fidelity, an unseemly scramble ensued between Stravinsky and Monteux as to who should be the first to issue an orchestral recording. This was in 1929. Other conductors followed suit, starting with Stokowski in 1930, until the *Rite* became the flagship of the record industry, one of the most recorded of twentieth-century works, and the benchmark by which all virtuoso orchestras were judged.

Stravinsky was one of the first composers, perhaps the first, to see the opportunity recording gave of extending his control over his music. He had a low opinion of orchestral musicians, and an even lower one of conductors. Again and again, in interviews and writings, he expressed the frustration of the creative artist whose work is distorted by an intermediary. As far as the *Rite* is concerned, Stravinsky's most important comments come in two collections of record reviews (published in

118

the books of conversations with Robert Craft) which are unsparing in their criticisms of leading conductors, himself included.[2]

As early as 1935 Stravinsky had set out his philosophy. Recording was a means of 'safeguarding [my] work by establishing the manner in which it ought to be played...' Recordings are 'documents' which can serve as guides to all executants of my music ... everyone who listens to my records hears my music free from any distortion of my thought, at least in its essential elements'.[3]

The conductor in the 1930s, taking Stravinsky at his word, could have consulted the 1929 recording, the first of three studio recordings made with the composer as conductor (the others date from 1940 and 1960). This 1929 version is, however, a far-from-ideal model: much of the playing is ragged, the difficult gear-changes are clumsily handled, and the faster tempi severely compromised by technical shortcomings. It should be said that the fault lies almost certainly with Stravinsky's conducting. The *Orchestre de Straram*[4] was a highly regarded ensemble (it was, incidentally, the Parisian orchestra preferred by Toscanini) whose repertoire was mainly contemporary; moreover the players were familiar with the *Rite*, having already given two concert performances under Stravinsky's baton.[5]

A much more reliable guide, despite its obvious limitations, was likely to have been the version for piano roll. The *Rite* was one of a number of Stravinsky works transcribed for the Pleyel company in the1920s.[6] A significant point to note is that in the piano roll version the music was not performed but transcribed direct from score to roll.[7] The laborious process has been described by Rex Lawson in the notes which accompany his pianola recording of the *Rite* – 'Typically, a music editor would place the sheet music on a small lectern in front of him and would lay a blank master roll across a table at which he sat. A scale of note lengths would be decided upon, perhaps 24 perforations to the beat, and the music would be marked up and then stamped out by hand, with a hammer and several sizes of punch.'[8] The work was supervised closely by Stravinsky, who occupied an apartment in the same building as the Pleyel premises.[9] Because the process was artificial, it therefore sidestepped the *Rite*'s notorious technical problems. The piano roll is thus likely to be a more accurate indication of Stravinsky's early performance intentions than the 1929 recording, at least as regards tempo and tempo relationships, the aspects of performance which Stravinsky regarded as paramount.[10]

In the following discussion I have assigned metronome values to the tempi of each performance. These are assembled in the grid (p. 124). In my text most metronome values are followed by a second figure in brackets, this being the tempo given in the final edition of the score (1967). These 1967 tempi are mostly the same as those in earlier editions, with one or two significant differences which I will highlight as they occur. I have used metronome values for the sake of precision and for greater ease of comparison. They are, however, approximate – especially in earlier performances of the *Rite* in which the notion of a fixed, invariable tempo for each section simply did not exist. This continuous flexibility is striking evidence of the general change in performance style since the 1920s; it may well also indicate that early performers regarded the *Rite*'s rhythms as melodic and gestural rather than mechanical.

The superiority of the piano roll version is apparent even in the 'Introduction', a section where instrumental timbres are needed to articulate the multitude of different lines. The control over rhythm and tempo creates a clear ternary shape, with the frame of the bassoon solo and its return (fig. 12) much slower than the central più mosso; in the latter the wind solos are sharply defined, characterised by a molto staccato touch. Both are features on which Stravinsky would later insist. In the 1929 orchestral recording the più mosso is rushed (crotchet = 72 [66]) and inflexible, so that the wind phrases are cramped and lacking in eloquence.

The transition before 'Augurs' (figs. 12–13) is odd in both versions. The implication of all editions of the score is that the tempo of 'Augurs' is set by the preceding pizzicato figure. In the piano roll these pizzicati continue at exactly the very slow tempo of the bassoon solo so that an abrupt gear-change is needed at the arrival of the repeated chords which open 'Augurs'. While one might attribute this to the inflexibility of the pianola medium, a similar clumsiness is also found in Stravinsky's recording with orchestra.

A unique feature of the 1929 recording is the tempo of 'Spring Rounds', where the pulse exactly matches that of 'Augurs'. This is a throwback to the conception in the original libretto whereby the two movements were adjacent.[11] Oddly, in the piano roll there is no attempt to establish this relationship; on the contrary, the tempo is both much slower than the printed score (crotchet = 70 [80]) and much slower than any other early recording.

In 'Ritual of Abduction', the *Rite*'s first great rhythmical challenge, the piano roll is strangely conservative in tempo (dotted crotchet = 120 [132]). Another intriguing difference with 1929 comes at the climactic confrontation at fig. 46, the point at which the 9/8 metre fragments into irregular bars of 3/8, 5/8, 4/8, etc. The piano roll is the only one of Stravinsky's performances to continue at quaver = quaver. The four-hand score of 1913 suggests that, whatever Stravinsky may have done later, this was indeed his original conception: by arranging the wood-wind and trumpet tune with the same tremolo writing as earlier in the movement Stravinsky implies that the tempo should remain constant.[12]

A real curiosity is the 1929 reading of 'The Sage', the four bars immediately before 'Dance of the Earth'. This is at more than twice the speed of the piano roll (crotchet = 88 [42]), and seems to be a throwback to the 1913 four-hand score, which sets the new quaver at the speed of the crotchets of the preceding molto allegro (crotchet = 168), giving almost exactly the tempo of the 1929 recording.

Not surprisingly it is the score's most problematic passage – the 'Sacrificial Dance' – which yields most insights. Again the two versions are at odds. The piano roll offers the sharpest contrast to modern performances where the ideal of achieving a rock-steady rhythm has come to mean a steady tempo, at or below the score's quaver = 126 (Rattle, for example, at quaver = 108). In the piano roll Stravinsky is at quaver = 138, with the coda (from fig. 186) even faster, at quaver = 152. By contrast, the penultimate section, the gathering of forces which begins with the timpani rampage at fig. 174, is markedly slower. This change of tempo goes right back to Stravinsky's earliest conception, manifest in the 1913 four-hand edition, where fig. 174 is marked sostenuto e maestoso (crotchet = 116). Oddly, in view of the performance on the piano roll, this instruction has disappeared by the time of the first printed orchestral score (1921). But the tradition lingered on in the performances of all the *Rite*'s pioneering conductors. To this Stravinsky in 1929 is the exception, presumably on account of his conservative

initial tempo. This point alone provides strong evidence that
Stravinsky's first version with orchestra was very far from his ideals.
Monteux 1929 may be used to arbitrate between the sharp discrepancies of the two Stravinsky versions.[13] In contrast to the confused picture
there, Monteux's is coherent and convincing and merits close attention
as the first outstanding version of the *Rite*. Monteux was an expert
conductor (as Stravinsky was not); his experience of the *Rite* was rooted
in the theatre, as is very evident from this recording; and he was trusted
by Stravinsky and imbued with Stravinsky's views, though by no means
a slave to them.

Very possibly Monteux in 1929 is a credible record of what the public
heard in 1913. He seems to have been a 'conservative' conductor – his
later recorded versions are in essential respects similar to the 1929
account – and he continued to prefer the first edition of the score. The
characteristic which chiefly distinguishes Monteux from modern conductors is the long-range shaping of the music through (often quite
slight) variations in pacing. Some of these are indicated in the score, of
course – as in the più mosso in the 'Introduction', under Monteux
sufficiently faster for the wind to chorus anarchically, but not rushed as
in Stravinsky 1929.

Others are on Monteux's initiative. In 'Augurs', for example, Monteux's tempo is 'monumental', only a shade faster than Stravinsky. But
where with Stravinsky the later stages of the movement drag, Monteux
releases momentum. This is done very precisely: at fig. 18 (the reprise of
the opening barrage of chords, before the exchanges between bassoons
and trombone), the performance vividly recalling Stravinsky's 'old
woman running ahead etc.'; and at the logically appropriate passage, the
transition (figs. 30–1) immediately after the 'Spring Rounds' premonition.

Also important is Monteux's handling of the slow music of the
opening to Part II, right up to the 'casting of lots'. Stravinsky regarded
this passage from the duet for two trumpets up to 'Glorification' as
containing the *Rite*'s weakest music – a view formed, perhaps, by
repeated shortcomings in performance.[14] Monteux's secret is again a
controlled (and again logical) unfolding of momentum. His opening,
nightmarishly atmospheric, is virtually half the speed of Stravinsky's
1929 performance (at crotchet = 42 [48]). The line is broken by the first

bar of the trumpet duet, standing out in relief (crotchet = 58); thus the point at which the two principal streams of music overlap is sharply delineated by differences in tempo.

A consequence is that the trumpets sound more urgent, less 'passive', than usual, and this in turn makes the ensuing tutti (fig. 87) dart and flicker. In keeping with this 'Mystic Circles' is a shade more lively than the score's crotchet = 60, and the problems of the tempo primo (fig. 97) – notoriously sticky in many modern performances – are briskly circumvented (crotchet = 76 [60]). Thus the pairs of crotchets have an urgent 'pleading', calmed by the quartet of horns (at fig. 99) as Monteux permits the music to expand. As Monteux's reading makes clear, this section is the nearest the *Rite* gets to outright description, the 'pantomime' that, in later years, Stravinsky said he wished to avoid.

Indeed the climax to Monteux's intensely dramatic account – and by far the most sensational aspect of this recording – is the 'Sacrificial Dance' – at quaver = 160, both confirming and surpassing the piano roll, and in total contrast with the 'monolithic' approach which is now the norm. And true to the tradition outlined earlier, Monteux broadens majestically in the penultimate section.[15]

The second part of this survey is based on recordings which range from among the earliest to the present day. The selection is based on the six performances reviewed by Stravinsky in later life.[16] These are conducted by Karajan 1963, Boulez 1963 and 1969, P. Крафт[17] with the USSR Symphony Orchestra 1962, Mehta 1970 and Stravinsky himself (1960). For purposes of comparison I have included a later recording by Karajan 1975. Important versions by Stokowski 1930 and Markevich 1951 are considered, and a more recent generation is represented by Rattle 1987. I have referred also to later recordings by Monteux, as well as by others who conducted the *Rite* in the 1920s (Ansermet and Goossens). Other conductors mentioned include Schuller 1971, together with recent recordings by Nagano 1990 and Craft 1995.

	Piano Roll 1921	Stravinsky 1929	Monteux 1929	Stokowski 1930	Stravinsky 1940	Markevich 1951	Stravinsky 1960	Craft 1962	Boulez 1963	Karajan 1963	Boulez 1969	Mehta 1970	Karajan 1975	Rattle 1987
'Introduction' ♩=50	♩=c.46	♩=52	♩=c.50	♩=52	♩=63	♩=48	♩=48	♩=46	♩=54	♩=56	♩=48	♩=46	♩=54	♩=44
Più mosso ♩=66	♩=60	♩=72	♩=60	♩=58	♩=70	♩=56	♩=66	♩=58	♩=58	♩=63	♩=52	♩=50	♩=58	♩=52-4
'Augurs' [13] ♩=50 [56]	♩=50 / ♩=92 [box]	♩=48	♩=50+	♩=54	♩=58	♩=54	♩=54	♩=50	♩=50	♩=48	♩=50	♩=60	♩=50	♩=54
'Ritual of Abduction' [37] ♩=132	♩=120	♩=138	♩=120	♩=132	♩=132	♩=126	♩=132	♩=116 (!)	♩=116	♩=144	♩=120	♩=120	♩=138	♩=132
[43] ♪=♪	♪=♪	♩=112	♩=116	♪=♪	♪=♪(!)	♩=116	♩=112	♩=100	♪=♪	♪=♪	♩=108	♩=112	♪=♪	♪=♪
Tranquillo [48] ♩=108	♩=104	♩=120	♩=104	♩=80	♩=108	♩=76	♩=116	♩=92	♩=100	♩=72-6	♩=104	♩=72	♩=66	♩=98
Sostenato [49] ♩=80 / Vivo [54] ♩=160	♩=70 ! / ♩=120	♩=96 ! / ♩=152	♩=80 / ♩=160	♩=84 / ♩=152	♩=78 / ♩=160	♩=60 / ♩=160	♩=80 / ♩=148	♩=63 / ♩=156	♩=68 / ♩=152	♩=66 / ♩=160	♩=58 / ♩=172	♩=56-8 / ♩=144	♩=60 / ♩=160	♩=74 / ♩=176
'Rival Tribes' [57] ♩=168	♩=160	♩=152	♩=152	♩=168	♩=168	♩=156	♩=148	♩=156	♩=168	♩=168	♩=152	♩=152	♩=144	♩=152
'Sage' [72▲] ♩=42	♩=40	♩=88 !	♩=46	♩=58	♩=52	♩=44	♩=40	♩=133 (!)	♩=52	♩=42	♩=56	♩=56	♩=40	♩=42
'Dance of the Earth' [72] ♩=168	♩=152	♩=150	♩=152	♩=168	♩=168	♩=160	♩=144	♩=160	♩=152	♩=160	♩=136	♩=152	♩=152	♩=168
Part II: 'Introduction' [79] ♩=48	♩=43 Più mosso (89) ♩=56	♩=76/8 ([box]=66)	♩=42 t'pets=58	♩=44	♩=48	♩=44 t'pets=50	♩=48	♩=46	♩=51	♩=46	♩=52	♩=52	♩=50	♩=44
'Mystic Circles' [91] ♩=60	♩=72	♩=60	♩=60	♩=69	♩=72	♩=66	♩=72	♩=60	♩=60	♩=56	♩=76	♩=76	♩=63	♩=66
Più mosso [93] ♩=80	♩=96	♩=92	♩=108	♩=92-6	♩=80	♩=92	♩=80	♩=92	♩=90	♩=100	♩=100	♩=116	♩=82	♩=120
Tempo 1 [97] ♩=60	♩=57	♩=63	♩=76	♩=72	♩=72	♩=60	♩=72	♩=60	♩=60	♩=60	♩=58	♩=60	♩=54-6	♩=72
'Glorification' [104] ♩+♪=144	♪+♪=144	♪+♪=112	♪+♪=138	♪+♪=132	♪+♪=138	♪+♪=132	♪+♪=144	♪+♪=132	♪+♪=138	♪+♪=144	♪+♪=132	♪+♪=148	♪+♪=136	♪+♪=130
'Evocation' [121] ♪=♪	l'istesso tempo	♩=92	♩=120	♩=100	♩=126	♩=112	♩=126 (!)	♩=120	l'istesso tempo	♩=112	l'istesso tempo	♩=120	l'istesso tempo	l'istesso tempo
'Ritual Action' [129] ♩=52	♩=54	♩=58	♩=68	♩=88	♩=69 (!)	♩=58	♩=63	♩=58-66	♩=69	♩=52	♩=58/60	♩=58	♩=56	♩=62
'Sacrificial Dance' [142] ♪=126	♪=138	♪=104	♪=160 !	♪=126	♪=120	♪=132	♪=126	♪=126	♪=126	♪=112	♪=116	♪=138	♪=126	♪=108
[149]	♪=138	♪=116	♪=144	♪=120	♪=132	♪=144	♪=132	♪=126	♪=136	♪=120	♪=126	♪=138	♪=126	♪=120
[167]	♪=138	♪=116	♪=160	♪=126	♪=120	♪=138	♪=126	♪=126	♪=136	♪=120	♪=126	♪=138	♪=126	♪=112
[174]	♩=126 !	♩=108	♩=108-116 !	♩=96!	♩=126	♩=126	♩=126	♩=120-126	♩=136	♩=116	♩=126	♩=138	♩=126	♩=132
[181] / [186]	♩=116 / ♪=152	♩=108 / ♪=112	♩=120 / ♪=152	♩=100 / ♪=116	♩=132 / ♪=126	♩=126 / ♪=138	♩=126 / ♪=128	♩=126 / ♪=120	♩=136 / ♪=136	♩=120 / ♪=126	♩=126 / ♪=126	♩=138 / ♪=138	♩=126 / ♪=126	♩=124 / ♪=124

Part I

Introduction

In the opening bars of the score three difficulties stand out: the tessitura and timbre of the bassoon solo; the rhythmic displacement of the second note (D) in the horn part, together with the indicated (intrusive) dynamic (*mp*); the poco accelerando, awkward for the clarinets since it is difficult to feel together and the conductor's beat can be of little assistance.

Mehta with the Los Angeles Philharmonic occupies the blandest end of the spectrum. The bassoon is 'saxophone-like and vibrato-shiny'[18] (Stravinsky's description of an earlier performance by Boulez (1963) applies equally here); moreover, the second horn note arrives together with (rather than before) the bassoon, 'a mistake that changes the whole character of the beginning'.[19] Finally, the accelerando is replaced by a ritardando.

These details are not a matter of carelessness. They reveal that Mehta has failed to appreciate a fundamental characteristic of the *Rite*. The point about the horn line is that it is emphatically not an accompaniment: instead it forms a quite distinct layer pointedly not co-ordinated with the bassoon. Similarly, the point of the poco accelerando is to work against (not with) the grain of the rhythm, providing a resistance to the natural tendency to taper the phrase-ending. Such sharply sculpted layering is the essence of the 'Introduction', which climaxes in the hardest 'edge' – the return of the bassoon solo (fig. 12), which resumes after the first of the *Rite*'s climactic gridlocks.[20]

Mehta is by no means unique. Similar faults are found in Boulez 1963 and Karajan 1963 – and if anything still more so in their later versions (1969 and 1975 respectively). Not surprisingly these openings presage performances of the 'Introduction' which are all similarly under-characterised. There is little change at the più mosso (after fig. 3), so that, as Stravinsky puts it, 'there is of course no return, with the bassoon (at fig. 12), to a tempo primo that was never departed from'.[21] Wind solos (such as the decisive oboe at fig. 9) are legato (where staccato is specified); and the half-asleep tempo common to all performances means that gestures such as the flute arpeggios into fig. 7 are unworkable (in Mehta these are actually played allargando).

By contrast, other versions are more 'gestural'. Markevich, with the Philharmonia Orchestra, takes a languorous approach, the atmosphere more weary than expectant, heavy with menace. The opening is 'distant' and meticulous, and already with the cor anglais solo (at fig. 2) the strategy is clear, this being held back, not urgent. The più mosso is very slight (crotchet = 56 [66]) and Markevich takes advantage of the additional space to characterise vividly individual phrases, marked often by tiny lingerings.

Stokowski 1930 interprets the più mosso not as a sudden gear-change but as initiating a gradual release of momentum – this reaches a settled plateau only at fig. 4 (the solos for oboe and piccolo clarinet): with Stokowski this becomes a key moment in the music's progression, an expressive flowering after the meticulously discrete fragments of the first page. Rattle, similarly, sees the più mosso (in itself hardly perceptible in his performance) as part of a continuing progression. His wind solos have a sly, insinuating character – compared with Stokowski's ecstatic 'swarm', Stravinsky's original word for this passage.[22]

Transition (figs. 12–13) and *Augurs of Spring*

Stravinsky's written comments reinforce intentions already clear from the score – the fragments of pizzicati should run at exactly the same tempo into fig. 13; and 'Augurs' should be held steady, as noted by Stravinsky in his review[23] of the USSR State Symphony Orchestra (incorrectly given in *Dialogues* as the Moscow State Symphony Orchestra) under the mysterious P. Крафт (a coy disguise for 'R. Craft').

Most performances follow the first instruction – but does Stravinsky? Certainly not, as we have seen, in the piano roll, nor in the orchestral version of 1929: in both the pizzicati are well below tempo. In 1940 the relationship is closer; closer still in 1960. Even so, Stravinsky, as conductor, seems to have thought of the pizzicati (whatever he may have said) as mediating between the bassoon – which is so rhapsodic as to be without defined tempo – and 'Augurs': a half-formed premonition, whose character emphasises the transitional nature of figs. 12–13.

The reverse of this is adopted (convincingly) by Stokowski: the pizzicati (together with the coruscating clarinet trill) are sharply auth-oritative, a sudden call-to-order – this is after all the *Rite*'s first tempo giusto. Thereafter, however, they are held back, so that a similar tempo to Stravinsky's for the repeated chords at fig. 13 – the down bows fiercely reiterated, with horns yelping like hunting dogs – is arrived at by the opposite means.

When 'Augurs of Spring' gets underway much depends on the choice of tempo. The score's minim = 50 is daringly steady. On the plus side it can make for hugely emphatic, even grotesque, opening chords (com-pare this with Mehta's effortless minim = 60). Furthermore, a 'gripped' tempo accords with a long-term shaping of Part I as a more or less continuous acceleration.

However this maestoso approach certainly creates problems later. Interestingly, Stravinsky's original conception seems to have been slightly quicker (minim = 56, as in the 1913 four-hand score). In later life, however, Stravinsky stood by the revised tempo (minim = 50).[24]

A steady minim = 50 might work if the legato melodies at fig. 25 (horn then flute) and again after fig. 28 (the trumpets' version of what will be the theme of 'Spring Rounds') can be kept buoyant – perhaps through hyperactive accompaniment: but the example of Karajan 1963, 1975 and Boulez 1969 is not encouraging. (See also, similarly, Stravinsky 1929 and the piano roll.)

Monteux (as we have seen) makes the printed tempo work through surreptitious flexibility. More commonly conductors favour a slightly livelier opening – as does Stravinsky 1940 and 1960. The danger – evident in both these Stravinsky versions – is that the movement 'jogs' a little too comfortably. Markevich keeps up the sense of urgency by pushing forward fractionally after the *cæsura* (before fig. 22); in this he is similar to Monteux, but begins from a more flowing tempo. Stokowski (at exactly Stravinsky's 1960 minim = 54) avoids stodginess through fierce characterisation, as for example in the down-bow gruppetti at fig. 23. Incidentally, Stokowski's performance for the sound-track of Dis-ney's *Fantasia* solves the problem of flagging momentum by deftly excising the transition which precedes the horn melody at fig. 25! The 'gestural' playing of Stokowski's orchestra contrasts with the rhythmic strictness of more modern performances; these seek to generate excite-ment through different means, the piling up of sharply-etched detail, so that, for example, the thrummed pizzicati (fig. 31) which bothered Stravinsky[25] can really be heard. Rattle, for example, at minim = 54 (the tempo of Stravinsky 1960 and of Stokowski) shows the benefits of the unwavering approach, culminating in a mesmerising *crescendo* (from fig. 32).

Ritual of Abduction

In this *tour de force* every section of the orchestra is – or should be – stretched to the limit. Why, then, is Boulez in both readings so cautious? (Mehta also) – the 1969 version being described by Stravinsky as 'perniciously slow'.[26] Stravinsky himself 1940 and 1960 takes the climactic passage at fig. 43 steadily, too steadily for any sense of struggle. Stokowski, by contrast, gives a fearless account, ripping through fig. 43 without hesitation, and maintaining the presto (as Stravinsky never did) through fig. 46 (see earlier discussion of this passage on p. 121). Rattle, all of a piece with his implacable climax to 'Augurs', again shows that a controlled approach can be turned to good account – stressing the antiphonal exchanges (which show the movement's kinship with 'Rival Tribes'); again the passage from fig. 47 (another gridlock) is implacable rather than impulsive.

Spring Rounds: tranquillo (fig. 48) and sostenuto e pesante (fig. 49)

As with the transition between the 'Introduction' and 'Augurs', this passage seems to open a 'window' – the melody, in its piercing, aquiline timbre, functions much as did the returning bassoon (at fig. 12). Stravinsky's comments on Mehta are revealing: 'The tranquillo is too slow ... [but] so is the dance proper too slow, as well as wrong in character – oversweet and lacking in edge.'[27] Stravinsky so rarely refers to 'character' that we may take it that the point has special importance: it is, surely, that the energy and tension (of the closing climax to 'Abduction') is set aside (temporarily), but not dissipated. In the early sketches, before Stravinsky had repositioned 'Ritual of Abduction' to come between 'Augurs' and 'Spring Rounds', the tranquillo was marked crotchet = 144. After the switch in the order, the tranquillo became a ready-made escape-hatch from the frenzied impasse which ends 'Ritual of Abduction'. In order to fulfil this new function Stravinsky drastically reduced the tempo, from 144 to 108. The briskness of the original conception is still apparent in Stravinsky's 1929 recording.

Unaccountably, both Stravinsky in 1940 and the piano roll make an allargando at the end of the transition. Similar pull-backs in Boulez 1963 were dubbed by Stravinsky as 'ugly solecisms'.[28] With Nagano the tempo is both slow and laden with rubato (minims become dotted minims) ending with a huge ritardando. If the tempo is slow, then the trick seems to reside in the trills, which must seem to 'condense' the energy of 'Ritual of Abduction' (see especially Monteux 1929). Stokowski manages a sense of suspended momentum – crotchet = 80 (108). Thus he reverses his earlier strategy (before 'Augurs') so that here the dance proper is faster than the preceding transition (here crotchet = 84).

With Mehta, the sostenuto e pesante is reduced to a funereal dirge (crotchet = 56–8, as also in both versions by Karajan) and an undignified one, too, with syrupy horns and a molto (not poco) ritardando before fig. 54 (the Vivo). Stokowski's articulation – long string crotchets – makes the *ff* (fig. 53) not brash but a powerful welling-up of previously suppressed feeling, played molto cantabile. By contrast, Stravinsky (leaving to one side the never-repeated 1929 experiment of playing 'Spring Rounds' at the same speed as 'Augurs') is dryer, in sound and in feeling: the strings' down bows are very detached – in contrast with molto legato horns – so that the melody floats descant-like above the trudge of the cantus firmus. Again we see the separation of layers as a way of avoiding, in slow tempi, the tendency for a fatal relaxation (Karajan, Boulez, Mehta and others).

A superb reading is by Markevich, in the tranquillo dry and remote (and perfectly in tune), and in the E♭ minor harmonies of the dance eschewing the sumptuous, glamorised sound (and tempo) of Karajan, Mehta or Nagano.

Rival Tribes

Remembering the headlong piano roll version (crotchet = 168–92) modern performances are usually slow. Karajan 1963 is the exception, at crotchet = 168 (his 1975 recording is at crotchet = 144). A slow tempo has two advantages: it assists a long-term progression – to a faster 'Dance of the Earth', and enhances the articulation – enabling, for instance, the staccato quavers ('daggers', Stravinsky called them[29]) before fig. 61 to be played with down bows. On the debit side, the orchestra has to work especially hard (as does the CBSO under Rattle) to articulate the struggle between the warring 'blocks'. Stokowski (no slave to the metronome) brings these to a head with a huge pull-back in the four bars before fig. 59.[30] Later the melodic thirds (figs. 61–2) can sound 'inappropriately lyrical':[31] they are indeed pretty, but only as a patch of blue glimpsed among thunderclouds.

Procession of the Sage

The clearer the 'rhythmic polyphony'[32] the greater the excitement. Rattle – uniquely – attends scrupulously to the reduced dynamic for the horns at fig. 66: *f ma non tanto* (with tubas already underway at *mf*). Fig. 66 onwards is thus played at what seems like an icy *quasi p* into which the hubbub at fig. 70 bursts with shattering force.

The Sage – Dance of the Earth

These are the sections most improved in Stravinsky's 1940 version – with 'Dance of the Earth' fast and disciplined. While no one approaches the speedy dispatch of 'The Sage' in Stravinsky's 1929 version, almost all are faster than Stravinsky would like – and in 'Dance of the Earth' almost always slower. Stravinsky himself (1960) is cautious ('too slow').[33] Karajan's early version (1963) is at this tempo, rescued by an accelerando, initially slight but ultimately all-consuming. By 1975 Karajan had formalised this so that the whole final fugato (from fig. 75) has a constant progressive acceleration. As an *étude* in double-tonguing it is magnificent (every syllable of the trumpets' semiquavers is audible) but dramatically and structurally flat. The opening (from fig. 72) – which in Karajan is maestoso – is related melodically to 'Rival Tribes' and rhythmically to the exasperated syncopations at the end of 'Abduction' – and should of course surpass both. Stravinsky is right, surely – 'a slightly faster tempo than the metronomic crotchet = 168 would not be amiss: it is not an allegro, after all, but a prestissimo.[34] It is left to Rattle to show that the former daring of Stokowski can be matched without compromising modern ideals of clarity.

Part II

Introduction

What might be termed the 'Romantic' approach is epitomised by Stokowski: the 'pushes' (as in bar 2) all very marked, the atmosphere brooding, with a subterranean shudder at fig. 80 (the D minor harmony) together with swooping portamenti. Above these, each woodwind chord reaches painfully for the next. The trumpets (fig. 84 + 4) are ideally distant, the phrases around fig. 85 laboured and sinister. The tutti elaboration of the trumpets' idea (fig. 87) is gashed by rapid clarinet arpeggios.[35] Goossens, a law unto himself, creeps through the 'Introduction' at crotchet = 38, with only a hair's-breadth increase for 'Mystic Circles' (crotchet = 40 [60]). Boulez 1969 is as evocative as Stokowski, but in a completely different way and by different means – not espressivo but through detail so meticulous as to be 'precious' (hence sinister).

Structurally there is a similarity with the 'Introduction' to Part I: the music juggles between 'future' and 'past', between premonition and recall – this is the implication of the tempo changes: fig. 89 looks forward (to 'Mystic Circles') while fig. 90 is a Stygian version of the earlier trumpet duet. Mehta seems oblivious to these nuances: there is no 'distancing' to the sound (trumpets), the section at fig. 87 'lacks accents, rhythmic articulation, tension',[36] and fig. 89 (the più mosso premonition of 'Mystic Circles') trundles at the same tempo. Stravinsky, it has to be said, is hardly better in 1940 or 1960. Ansermet, after an exquisite *ppp* before fig. 86, sees no urgency in the passage at fig. 87, initiated slackly by a clarinet arpeggio which is at half speed. Rattle as always is interesting: his wind chords at the opening have not the eloquence of Stokowski (nor of Monteux) but he also is prepared to risk a very slow tempo, laden moreover with rubato – in a languorous tapering of the 'push' motif, and in easing the ends of diminuendi: thus the three-times repeated D minor harmonies are hieratic in their insistence. There is space and distance in the exchanges (strings/trumpets) around fig. 85; fig. 87 (the tutti) is on tip-toes, finding drama in the balance between twinkling detail and the impersonal duet (here horn/clarinets).

Mystic Circles

Here early interpreters are wary of the score's very slow tempi, especially the return to crotchet = 60 at fig. 97 (the tempo of the opening melody at fig. 91). Monteux 1929, as we have seen, though slow at fig. 91, frankly ignores tempo primo: his version (at fig. 97) is more agitated than hypnotic, an advantage being that this permits an eloquent relaxation where the music dwells on the 'Mystic Circles' theme (beginning with the quartet of horns, from fig. 99). Rattle is very similar in approach. By the same token almost all performances treat the middle section of the music's 'three-part shape'[37] as agitato, much quicker than the score's crotchet = 80.

Can the conception implied by the score's metronome marks (crotchet = 60 ... 80 ... 60) be made to work? The nearest to the letter is Karajan – particularly 1975 (più mosso at crotchet = 82) – but both his readings, sumptuous and meticulous though they may be, are enervatingly undramatic, with no sense of impending catastrophe: the exchanges at fig. 99, with the subsequent 'casting of lots', seem interminable. One explanation is the lack of 'bite': the texture at fig. 91, for example, where the much-heralded 'Mystic Circles' melody at last arrives, is homogeneous – nothing is made of the 2/4 pizzicati and their potential as an acerbic, destabilising undercurrent. Nagano is more flowing here, but 'returns' to a much slower tempo primo (at fig. 97) which is exactly at the score's crotchet = 60. More characterful is Ansermet, his (rather unsteady) pizzicato syncopations at fig. 97 limping grotesquely.

A workable compromise (at fig. 97) between Monteux/Stokowski and Karajan/Ansermet is Schuller, who with a student orchestra achieves a miracle of continuity throughout the opening pages of Part II (possibly a benefit of a 'live' rather than studio recording), at fig. 97 the score's crotchet = 60 eased fractionally, but without any sense of rush. A unique detail (indicative of the sensitivity of this performance) is the second 'tocsin', a little brighter and more 'forward' in its re-orchestration with trumpets.

Transition (figs. 102–4), Glorification and Evocation

This is one of the *Rite*'s most awkward passages: the reiteration (syncopated and with accelerando) slithering unstoppably into the 'orchestral haemorrhage' at fig. 103 and the hammered 11/4 bar from which 'Glorification' is released.

Ansermet begins subito più mosso (see also Mehta, and Monteux 1929) but without further acceleration, so that the 11/4 has to be another subito più mosso. Boulez 1963 is the opposite, forced to steady at the 11/4 having, as Stravinsky observes,[38] overshot the tempo. Karajan 1975 makes a positive, exaggerated feature of the same gesture, his repeated chords suddenly and grandly molto meno mosso. Rattle, having engineered a slow-starting and progressive accelerando, overshoots to crotchet = 130 (120) at the 11/4, then ignores the indicated gear-change into the Vivo.

The exact relationship between 'Glorification' and 'Evocation' became another Stravinsky *bête noire*. He insists repeatedly that the ideal version follows the letter of the score, whereby the pulse of 'Glorification' equals that of 'Evocation'. Boulez 1969 is 'perfect – exactly the way the music should be performed'.[39] In this Stravinsky was true to his earliest conception: the piano roll is exactly similar. Boulez is 'perfect' in tempo, but also ideal in the characterful quintet of bassoons (at fig. 125).

One could argue, however, that played this way 'Evocation' fights against its 'natural' tempo, lacking a necessary decisiveness (as well as grandeur). That indeed may be the point of Stravinsky's marking. As we have seen, a similar perverseness explains the difficulties with establishing the tempo of 'Augurs', whose minim = 50 is 'unnatural' in its slowness. Evidently in his performances Stravinsky was unable entirely to shake off his instinct to adopt a broader tempo, whatever his conscious intentions. His 1929 recording (as noted earlier) is massively maestoso, but even in 1940 'Evocation' is proportionally slower than the much faster 'Glorification'; and, amazingly, in 1960 the difference is even more pronounced – 'I dislike both [my] slow tempo ... and the ritenuto at the end, but was not aware of either when the recording was made.'[40]

It is clear that all the conductors have given the problem thought, and the range of solutions is intriguing. Mehta is the least subtle: after a tearaway (and rushed) 'Glorification', his 'Evocation' is much slower – but undeniably impressive (as with Stravinsky 1929) especially in its characterisation of stillness. The others attempt in different ways to have the best of both approaches. Either they reduce the tempo a shade at 'Evocation', so that the spirit if not exact letter of the score is followed – as do Monteux 1929 and Schuller; or they apply the slower tempo that 'works' for 'Evocation' also to the preceding 'Glorification'. A most exact compromise is struck by Karajan 1975 to thrilling effect (in both sections his pulse = 136 [144]). Craft 1995 is similar, at 132/130 (144). Rattle, whose cool and calculated approach is the mirror-image of the impulsive Mehta, is more obvious, but no less effective. His earlier refusal to increase the tempo after the 11/4 bar looks in retrospect like a deliberate strategy, and one with long-term implications: indeed giving a shape to Part II whereby 'Glorification' is not a sudden eruption, but absorbed as smoothly as possible into a continuity. The character of Rattle's 'Glorification' is also unusual: in his sturdy tempo the section has a grotesqueness not found in other versions.

Ritual Action

The question facing all conductors is whether this movement works at the score's painfully slow crotchet = 52?

To answer this one has to look to modern performances – earlier this was simply never attempted. Monteux 1929 – at crotchet = 68 (52) – is full of suppressed urgency, with no attempt at hypnotic stillness, Stokowski still more urgent (crotchet = 88). Interestingly, both Monteux 1929 and Stravinsky1940 arrive at a tempo for 'Ritual Action' which more or less follows l'istesso tempo from 'Evocation' (old minim = new quaver). (This applies not only to performances which hold back 'Evocations'. Boulez 1963 makes the same relationship, and since he is metronomically up to tempo in 'Evocation', in 'Ritual Action' he is thus 40 per cent or so over tempo.) In Stravinsky 1960 this is calibrated very exactly (minim/quaver = 126), presumably intentionally.

But can a genuinely slow 'Ritual Action' work? Stravinsky evidently doubts it. On Karajan 1963, he says – 'Whether or not metronomically correct, this *tempo di hoochie-koochie* is definitely too slow, and at 138 [the climax] the music is duller than Disney's dying dinosaurs.'[41] But Karajan 1975 shows it can be done. The alto flute is poised, the tone 'smoky' ; the dynamics meticulously layered (the detached cor anglais notes at fig. 131); the upward gruppetto on cor anglais (and later bass trumpet) again exact (not as so often – Mehta, for example – perfunctory or 'fudged'). The performance allows, even compels, the listener's ear to refocus (after the assault of 'Glorification'), to become alert to the tiniest detail. With such a background, the climaxes have epic inevitability, with perfect stillness regained at fig. 139 after the *Rite*'s most ruthless cut-off. Boulez 1969 attempts almost this tempo (slightly faster at crotchet = 58–60) but with limp results.

Rattle is appreciably 'easier' (crotchet = 62, thus almost l'istesso tempo with his 'Evocation'), but like Karajan gains from immaculate details: these include two unique features: the slither (after fig. 135) is frankly double-dotted; and (at last!) the trumpets at fig. 132 are lontano. Oddly Stravinsky had in mind something more sprightly: 'I do not like this passage played legato.'[42]

Sacrificial Dance

This is the section in which a change in performance ideals (compared with the 1920s) is most apparent. The tradition (noted earlier) of a rapid tempo – with variations in order to characterise subsections – has disappeared. New traditions, however, have emerged. One is at the opening, where for the syncopated chords (in the three bars after the initial pause) more recent performances respect the difference between semiquaver and quaver, thus progressing through the pattern short–longer–longest.[43] A pioneer in this respect is the magnificent account by Markevich, whose technical excellence is underlined by the fact that the Philharmonia achieves this nuance despite a tempo which (by more recent standards) is rapid (quaver = 132, rising to 144). Otherwise an attempt is apparent in Ansermet and in Stravinsky 1960, and is clearly achieved in Karajan 1975, then exaggerated by Rattle (enabled by his very sturdy [quaver = 108] opening tempo).

Figs. 149–167

Rattle is all but alone in articulating the 'cells' which are suggested by the score's beaming and phrase-marks. The cell idea, incidentally, was simply abandoned by Stravinsky in his 1943 revision in favour of making this notorious trap for the unwary easier to read.[44]

A unique, thrilling, feature of Stokowski is the additional emphasis (a slight holding-back) at fig. 159, revealing this passage for what it is, the climax to the 'push' motif *idée fixe* (which originates at the very beginning of Part II). Markevich, seemingly with the same end in view, adopts the opposite practice, driving forward ever more furiously (quaver = 152 [126]).

While most conductors take the accelerando in the last two bars (before fig. 167) as the score's way of warding off any allargando, the instruction is seized on to sudden and electrifying effect by Rattle. Boulez 1969 extends the accelerando as far back as fig. 159 (as a result this climax sounds skimped, the antithesis of Stokowski) so that fig. 166 hurtles at crotchet = 144 – a device condemned as 'deplorable'.[45]

First coda (from fig. 174)

Rattle goes some way to resuming the abandoned tradition, paradoxically by inverting former practice, so that the passage is actually faster (crotchet = 132 [126]).

Second coda (fig. 186 onwards)

Mehta, after a ruthless gallop through the 'peroration' (compare this with the real intoxication of, say, Monteux 1929) vitiates all excitement through lack of dynamic contrast, a common failing. In this respect, Monteux is greatly helped by retaining the original pizzicati (at fig. 186) – still apparent in his later recordings. This was technically the most hazardous passage for early orchestras (Stokowski, sadly, is at sea here): the first rock-steady version is by Markevich, and then Stravinsky (1960) himself. This granitic ideal, being simply not available to earlier conductors, the most effective is Monteux 1929 who permits an accelerando over the last two pages, in tandem with the score's *poco a poco crescendo* (from just before fig. 199).

Alas the ideal of steadiness and implacable force often takes precedence over any characterising of the 'cells', from whose juxtapositions the music derives its energy – an example is Boulez 1969.

Two conductors have evidently pondered the ending, with its potential for anticlimax. Ansermet adds a rhetorical portato to the syncopated chord which precedes the hushed runs on flutes; and Boulez 1969 massively separates the final chord from its anacrusis – thus, according to Stravinsky 'turning a not-very-good-idea into a vulgar one'.[46]

In the opening section of this survey, I left our imaginary conductor no doubt thoroughly confused by the discrepancies between Stravinsky in 1929 and the Stravinsky of the piano roll. Better advice would have been to listen to Monteux's recording, almost certainly the most authentic guide to Stravinsky's earliest intentions. When, later, one adds to these Stravinsky's subsequent versions (1940 and 1960), the picture presented by his recordings becomes not clarified but more confused. Attempt a comparison of all the Stravinsky sources – his own recordings, the various editions of the score (described by Louis Cyr as 'l'imbroglio presque inextricable'[47]), and Stravinsky's written views on how the work should be performed – and one finds that all frequently contradict one another. Moreover it is often on matters on which Stravinsky is most insistent that he most differs in his own recordings.

By becoming a conductor as well as a composer, Stravinsky could no longer maintain that there was only one right way to perform his music. Like all performers, over the years his interpretations changed, reflecting both changes in himself and in the orchestras he conducted. Nonetheless it was years before he would modify his stance. As late as 1954 he claimed that as a result of recording, 'In future there will be no doubt as to how [my music] should be played.'[48] A decade later, admitting perhaps that some of his recordings were less exemplary than others – '...even the poorest are valid readings to guide other performers'.[49] Eventually disillusion set in, Stravinsky confessing in 1968 – 'I have changed my mind ... about the advantages of embalming a performance on tape ... one performance represents only one set of circumstances.'[50]

If the case of the *Rite* illustrates why Stravinsky's hopes for the gramophone industry ended in disillusion, its central position in the record catalogue makes it a paradigm for the way tastes and techniques in performance changed in the twentieth century. The pioneering conductors who recorded the *Rite* had all learned the work in the theatre, or at least thought of it as dramatic. In time, with concert performances far outnumbering ballet productions, a more abstract view prevailed. This was encouraged by Stravinsky. First there were his well-publicised remarks on 'expression' in music, together with his suspicion that 'interpretation' meant distortion. More specifically, there was Stravinsky's disavowal of the libretto of the *Rite*, a process which can be traced through the *Montjoie!* affair, the triumph of the 1914 concert performance, and Stravinsky's misleading public relations on behalf of the supposedly abstract revival by Massine in 1920.

Despite the hostility of respected critics (even as late as the 1920s) the *Rite* became established, and matured from *enfant terrible* to a worshipped and much-analysed icon of modernism. The history of recording shows that as a work becomes better known, and available in more and more versions, so the selling-point becomes less the work than the performance. The *Rite* exemplifies this process, the gradual change from a contemporary work, regarded as well-nigh impossible to play, to 'classic'.

The advent of stereo led to a flood of new recordings, with the *Rite* a showpiece for state-of-the-art technique and technology. This was not always in the best interests of the music. While these recordings were marketed on the reputations of conductor and orchestra, there were ominous signs of gimmickry or caricature (as we have noted in versions by Boulez, Karajan, Mehta and Nagano), in sharp contrast with, for example, the unmannered approach of Markevich a decade earlier (1951). No wonder Stravinsky was moved to launch a bitter diatribe in his two spoof record reviews, of which the first (in *Dialogues*) ends – 'None of the three performances is good enough to be preserved.'[51]

Despite the need to individualise performances for marketing purposes, a comparison between the pioneer performances and succeeding generations reveals a marked loss of character. One would have thought it impossible to reduce the *Rite* to dullness, but some of the performances discussed here succeed triumphantly. It is understandable that the 'Russianness' has gone – mourned by Stravinsky – and the sense of the theatre. More worrying is the lack of overall grasp or purpose. In part this is a symptom of a profound change. Conductors of the generation of Monteux and Stokowski 'became' the composer, in the sense that in performance they assumed full responsibility for the musical experience. But reduce the conductor's status – as Stravinsky encouraged – and this sense of total responsibility disappears. At the same time, again in line with Stravinsky's thinking, the score shifts from being a symbolic 'representation' of the music, towards being regarded as a set of instructions which need only be followed for the music to result. All this helps to explain the air of complacency in many post-1960 recordings, not excluding Stravinsky himself. The enigma is Boulez, who has an unrivalled prestige in a work which he seems neither to like nor understand.

Fortunately we have at least one modern version which reveals the *Rite* as a great architectural – one might say 'symphonic' – statement. Whether or not one likes every detail of Rattle's performance with the CBSO – one might question the rubato-laden opening to Part II, for example – there is never any doubt that everything serves a compelling overarching strategy.

Two performances, however, stand out, representative of two very different but equally valid approaches to performing the *Rite*. Markevich and the Philharmonia, in 1951, personify the ideal of the unmannered, 'uninterpreted' performance set out by Stravinsky in his writings. Markevich has clearly thought deeply about the difficult decisions facing the conductor, and his solutions are so deft and musical that his intervention passes unnoticed. The playing is beautiful, the detail of the score attended to with the greatest care, so that technical standards surpass most recent performances; but the work loses nothing in excitement for being presented without exaggeration or gimmickry.

At the other end of the spectrum is Craft with the USSR State Symphony Orchestra, recorded in 1962 at a concert given in Stravinsky's presence. The orchestra sounds as though it has just encountered the *Rite* and is thrilled with the discovery.[52] Brilliant though the players are, there is not the slightest interest in the well-blended sheen of Western orchestras. Instead every wind solo in the 'Introduction' is exultantly declaimed, setting the stage for a performance epic in its grandeur and intensity. In this performance the *Rite* seems reborn, to have recaptured the shattering newness of 1913. Yet at the same time its most impressive characteristic is the way the performance emphasises the traditions from which the *Rite* sprang, the traditions of Russian art music and folk music which are so clearly in the players' blood.[53]

9

Conclusion

A principal aim of this book has been to try to find some explanation for the *Rite*'s extraordinary power, which for most listeners remains undiminished despite long familiarity. The reasons for this power are many and complex, but a key element is the subtlety with which Stravinsky 'seeds' decisive moments. Once one begins to see the music in terms of cause and effect, one can start to understand its momentum and see the *Rite* less as a series of explosive effects and much more as a developing continuity.

All music – and the *Rite* is no exception – tends to be remade in a way that reflects the era of its performer. In most performances of the *Rite* the work remains a collage of unmotivated if spectacular events, lacking the gripping sense of evolution conveyed by early recordings. Very possibly behind this lies the prevailing analytic and historical conception of the *Rite* as being constructed of static blocks, a narrow view which this book has attempted to question. Certainly the vast literature on the *Rite* hardly mentions Stravinsky's architectural achievement: his ideas and techniques are discussed out of context with little or no attention paid to the music's architecture, in reality one of the work's most fascinating aspects and the one which explains its mesmerising hold on the listener. The cause of this omission lies in the traditional critical view which classifies the *Rite* as a 'pure' example of early twentieth-century modernism, with Stravinsky represented as working in total reaction to all musical precedent. Despite the recent work on Stravinsky's origins, this dogma seems obstinately entrenched – all but set in stone.

When architecture is discussed it is in terms which are almost entirely negative. Even Taruskin unequivocally toes the orthodox line when it comes to the music itself, despite his exhaustive research into the *Rite*'s dramatic and musical sources. The *Rite*, he says, consists of 'static blocks' which progress (if they progress at all) through 'repetition, alternation, and – above all – sheer inertial accumulation... There would be no harmonic *progression*, no thematic or motivic *development*, no smoothly executed *transitions*... The only process that remained would be that of accumulation... A chord that in Rimsky-Korsakov could justify its existence only by "cunning preparation and resolution," by the process of its becoming and its proceeding, could now simply *be*.' Each chord or motif was 'so fixed that even transposition – let alone transformation or transition – were inconceivable'. Following another ancient dogma, Taruskin argues that the *Rite* was composed in a deliberate rejection of the German symphonic tradition which is supposed to have bedevilled Russia's greatest composers, Tchaikovsky among them; and that, in contrast to *Firebird* in which he had pursued the fetish of thematic unity, Stravinsky now becomes more and more 'antisymphonic' as work on the *Rite* proceeds.[1]

There is a gleam of fanaticism in all this, as well as the difficulty which an insufficiently critical acceptance of entrenched interpretative ideas always entails. The *Rite* was not composed as a cornerstone of twentieth-century music, nor even as a piece of music pure and simple, but as a piece of theatre. Stravinsky was born and bred for the theatre; and thanks to the experience of his work on *Firebird* and *Petrushka*, by the time of the *Rite* he knew exactly how to get the effects he wanted, which he would measure to the nearest millimetre.

What is so curious about the new Stravinsky scholarship is that, while every other myth has been challenged, the purely musical myth has been left in peace. The characteristics listed by Taruskin are important, of course, but on their own they are a very partial account of the music. There is so much more to the music of the *Rite*, not buried deeply, but on the surface of the score, for anyone to hear and see. Indeed there *are* transitions – one is even specified in a letter from Stravinsky to Roerich – passages which, as they hold in balance ideas-which-have-been with ideas-which-are-to-come, positively quiver with expectation. The *Rite* most certainly does have melodic purpose and consistency – that surely governed much of what Stravinsky did with his borrowed folk material – and, at least in Part II and the 'Introduction' to Part I, ideas do develop.

The big moments make their effect because of their very carefully engineered context. The effect of the *Rite* may be primitive, but the means to this end were sophisticated in the extreme.

Far from being a loose or episodic structure, the *Rite* is formally very strong – so strong that it could stand alone as a concert item, without any programme, and without being adapted into a suite of musical highlights. When Stravinsky heard of Diaghilev's intention to make cuts for the 1913 London performances he reacted with horror.

Taruskin's 'proof' that the *Rite* is 'antisymphonic'[2] is that Stravinsky was able, at a fairly late stage, to switch the order of movements in Part I.[3] Yes: but not without loss – the abandoning of the smooth acceleration which was the original conception – and at the expense of much additional stitching, some of which still shows. Apply Taruskin's litmus test to Part II and one finds the very opposite of what he intends: to switch a single phrase, much less a whole section, would be unthinkable. Stravinsky goes to immense trouble to tie everything in with the whole, even a sudden eruption like 'Glorification of the Chosen One' whose ideas are made to overlap with the music on either side. And when one considers the care with which Stravinsky grafts on to his structure the (originally unforeseen) 'Sacrificial Dance' – balancing it with a whole new opening section to the 'Introduction' – his thinking may reasonably be described as organic. To say that Part II 'becomes less not more architectonic'[4] is simply not true, when one remembers the patient evolution which is the most potent source of its power – and, moreover, this is a process not dreamed up by a later analyst but which is explicitly there in Stravinsky's sketches.

It is my contention that the *Rite*'s roots go well beyond the historicism with which Roerich and Stravinsky engaged with its subject matter, or the folk music which permeates the score. Throughout one finds innovation side by side with techniques which are from the traditions of music in which Stravinsky was brought up and trained – as when, in the 'Sacrificial Dance', in music so unfamiliar that Stravinsky could not at first write it down, the progress of the music is measured by (of all things!) a dominant pedal, itself the result (*pace* Taruskin) of a transposition of earlier material. One is tempted to say that Stravinsky deliberately balanced his most radical departures by anchoring them in the familiar, except that we need to remember that Stravinsky was writing music, not music history – and if a 'dominant pedal' would be useful, then he would use it. One of the delights of the sketches is that they enable us to follow his entirely pragmatic mind: for Stravinsky anything and everything was grist to his mill provided he could make it work. Despite his pragmatism, Stravinsky's music is marked – as Taruskin aptly puts it – by 'colossal authenticity'.[5] It is this that makes it truly revolutionary, not the details of its vocabulary which have caught the eye of composers or analysts. Stravinsky's total identification with his subject prompted the desire, at all costs, to avoid any hint of cultural tourism. The folk tunes had to be purged of folkiness, of sentiment; used neither as quotation, nor as model for pastiche, but transformed and absorbed – just as Roerich and Stravinsky aimed to present (not 'represent') the rituals of spring games and sacrifice. Similarly the stylistic features borrowed from folk music are exaggerated and totally transformed – whether the thrumming ostinati or drones, still discernible in 'Augurs of Spring' for example, or the lilt of an occasional change of metre (a characteristic of Russian folk music) which in Stravinsky prompts the *Rite*'s most famous rhythmic innovation, used to spectacular effect in the orgiastic metric irregularities of 'Glorification' or the 'Sacrificial Dance'.

In this, the *Rite* is a supreme manifestation of *stikhiya*, the elemental quality extolled by the poet Alexander Blok (in an influential essay published in 1908) in contrast with the constantly shifting, artificial culture (*kul'tura*) of modern society and its intelligentsia.[6] In this very particular Russian sense, the *Rite* is hardly art at all; and significantly, as we have seen with the *Montjoie!* affair, Stravinsky detested the language of art criticism. No wonder the cultured Parisian audience found it too strong to stomach; and no wonder that a grasp of the whole was beyond the post-war generation of the avant-garde, with its seers, acolytes and temples (Darmstadt, Donaueschingen, IRCAM), whose interest was confined to details of the *Rite*'s techniques.

In another sense this lack of overt expressiveness, of 'pity' – a feature which struck its earliest commentators – is part of the work's big idea: a drama beyond good or evil, beyond the strivings of free will, a drama of life lived in instinctive acceptance, whether of the forces of nature or of the spirits. In a tradition that can be traced back to J. J. Rousseau, Roerich would have seen this as a 'paradise lost' (as in the painting from the Ashmolean). Stravinsky, in a gloomy way that we can recognise as explicitly 'Russian' in works by Lermontov, Dostoevsky and Tolstoy, was more callous: he seems to say that we must accept those forces (nature, death) which because they terrify us, we try to control – is this perhaps why the *Rite*, perhaps more than any other piece of Western music, is so *frightening?* For Stravinsky, as we can see in later works like *Les Noces*, *L'Histoire du Soldat* and *Oedipus Rex*, the implacable momentum with which fate drives us through life is one of the great emotional wonders, a source of awe and, especially, a source of inspiration.

If such was the idea in Stravinsky's mind, whether conscious or not, it provides a further explanation of his need to dehumanise his folk sources. His means of doing this was to make his music – together with the human figures on stage – behave like machines in a way that seemed 'modern' to his contemporaries. Thus what purported to be a stone-age ballet could also be prophetic of the modern world – of war, destruction, of life dehumanised.

With the *Rite* music returned (albeit only in imagination) to its roots, not detached from life itself or placed in a shrine (the concert hall). The 'colossal authenticity' is the complete bonding of the music with the dramatic vision – so complete that in the end, by a strange unforeseen paradox which suddenly hit Stravinsky on the night of the *Rite*'s terrible première, the music could work without stage or scenario. The *Rite* is the first in a long line of Stravinsky's ritualised dramas; but unlike its successors it needs no 'frame', no theatrical artifice. Indeed, of all Stravinsky's stage works it is the most naturalistic: it has no narrator (as in *L'Histoire du soldat* or *Oedipus Rex*), no play-within-a-play (*Petrushka*), above all no pastiche (*Pulcinella*). Almost uniquely, the style of the music belongs to Stravinsky alone. Perhaps it is significant that this brutal chill comes when for the first time Stravinsky was not working harnessed to an experienced man from the ballet world, as he had been with Fokine and Benois (*Firebird* and *Petrushka*): now, for the first time, he was working with a new spirit, Nijinsky, who despite or perhaps because he was considerably younger than the composer could translate Stravinsky's vision into movement of complementary violence.

And so the *Rite* brought to a climax Stravinsky's musical adolescence, with the brilliance of sudden maturity after years as a dutiful student. He remembered 'the violent Russian spring that seemed to begin in an hour and was like the whole earth cracking – that was the most wonderful event of every year of my childhood'.[7] This was Stravinsky's springtime, when everything was ideally propitious: the influence and inspiration of Diaghilev and his company, the confidence born of sudden and great success, the delay of a year – the year of *Petrushka* – in which the *Rite* could germinate. And fate – or luck or inspiration – had presented him with the perfect subject. No wonder anything seemed possible, anything could be dared.

Even so, however much one seeks to explain it, the *Rite* seems inexplicable. For many of us the achievement of the *Rite* is that it just exists, a monumental presence, arousing the same feelings of impersonal wonder as the grandest works of nature. Stravinsky must have felt this too, that he 'discovered' the *Rite* rather than invented it – 'I heard, and I wrote what I heard. I am the vessel through which the *Rite* passed.'[8]

Notes

1 Origins

1 Igor Stravinsky and Robert Craft, *Expositions and Developments*, London, 1959 (1962), p. 140. Hereafter, *Expositions*.
2 *Comœdia Illustré*, 11 December 1920, quoted in Minna Lederman (ed.), *Stravinsky in the Theatre*, New York, 1949 (1975), p. 24.
3 Letter to Nikolai Findeyzen, editor, *Russian Musical Gazette*, 2/15 December 1912 in Appendix to *The Rite of Spring: Sketches 1911–1913*, London, 1969, p. 32. Hereafter, *Sketches*.
4 André Schæffner, *Strawinsky*, Paris, 1931, p. 35, quoted in Richard Taruskin, *Stravinsky and the Russian Traditions*, 2 vols., Oxford, 1996, I, p. 862. This is my translation of the French original.
5 *Chroniques de ma vie*, 1935, translated as *Chronicle of My Life*, London, 1935, and reprinted as *An Autobiography*, London, 1935 (1975), p. 31.
6 'Stravinsky seems to have almost total recall of his intensely active, creative, and usually technicolor dreams . . . the origins of many of his compositions have been in dreams as well as the solutions of musical problems.' From Robert Craft's diary, 2 July 1949, in Vera Stravinsky and Robert Craft, *Stravinsky in Pictures and Documents*, New York, 1978, p. 384. Hereafter, *Pictures and Documents*.
7 In one respect – the idea of a specifically spring ritual – Stravinsky's memory was certainly at fault. 'At the start of the ballet it is a summer night, and it ends with the sunrise, with the first rays of the sun', *St Petersburg Gazette*, 28 August 1910, quoted in Bronislava Nijinska, *Early Memoirs*, London, 1982, p. 448.
8 Letter to Nikolai Findeyzen, 2/15 December 1912, *Sketches*, Appendix, p. 32.
9 Letter to Nikolai Roerich 19 June/2 July 1910 (*Sketches*, Appendix, p. 28). Richard Taruskin has suggested that the sketches contained two themes, originally intended for the *Rite*'s 'Ritual of Abduction', which found their

way into the 'Danse Russe' from *Petrushka*. Taruskin, *Russian Traditions*, p. 709.

10 See Richard Buckle, *Diaghilev*, London, 1979, p. 167.

11 Alexander Benois, *Reminiscences of the Russian Ballet*, trans. Mary Britnieva, London, 1941, p. 347.

12 N. K. Rerikh, *Iz literatur-nogo naslediya*, p. 361, quoted in Jacqueline Decter, *Nicholas Roerich: The Life and Work of a Russian Master*, London, 1989, p. 89. *The Forefathers* (tempera on canvas) is in the Ashmolean Museum, Oxford. Its subject has been interpreted as a Russian counterpart of the myth of Orpheus by Serge Ernst – see Larissa Salmina-Haskell, *Russian Paintings and Drawings in the Ashmolean Museum*, Oxford, 1989, p. 73.

13 Design for the Polovstian Dances, pastel and pencil on reddish paper, Ashmolean Museum, Oxford.

14 Buckle, *Diaghilev*, p. 142.

15 Taruskin, *Russian Traditions*, p. 860.

16 Roerich, 'Radost' iskusstvu' pp. 531–2, quoted in Taruskin, *Russian Traditions*, p. 861.

17 Jacqueline Decter, *Nicholas Roerich*, p. 83.

18 The information comes from an interview between Roerich and an earlier biographer, Barnett Conlan. The relevant passage is quoted in Taruskin, *Russian Traditions*, p. 864, where the question of the original authorship of the *Rite* is discussed at length.

19 Craft, with uncharacteristic venom, describes Roerich as 'this monumental con artist', adding that his 'veracity is nearly always in question'. Robert Craft, *Glimpses of a Life*, London, 1992, p. 247, n. 1. The need for secrecy arose from the quarrel during the production of *Firebird* between Diaghilev and Fokine, the likely choreographer of the *Rite*. Indeed Fokine was approached, since by the end of July 1910 a second libretto 'worked out with Fokine' (and presumably with ideas for the choreography) was in existence. See letter from Stravinsky to Roerich, 27 July 1910, in *Sketches*, Appendix, p. 29.

20 Details of this are in Taruskin, *Russian Traditions*, pp. 662–3, also *Pictures and Documents*, p. 612, where Mask is spelt Masque. Also letter to Roerich (*Sketches*, Appendix, pp. 27–8).

21 As Taruskin observes 'the idea of a culminating sacrificial dance by the *prima ballerina* could only have occurred to someone steeped in the traditions and cliches of the romantic musical theater. That describes Stravinsky, not Roerich.' Taruskin, *Russian Traditions*, p. 864.

22 *Sketches*, Appendix, p. 29.

23 Stravinsky, *An Autobiography*, p. 31.
24 *Pièce Burlesque* is given as the original title in a note written by Stravinsky in October 1928 to accompany the pianola version of *Petrushka*. See *Pictures and Documents*, p. 67.
25 Buckle, *Diaghilev*, p. 179.
26 L. S. Dyachkova with B. M. Yarustovsky, ed., *I. F. Stravinskiy: stat'i i materiali*, Moscow, 1973, quoted in Taruskin, *Russian Traditions*, p. 680.
27 Letter to Roerich 2 (15) July 1911, in *Sketches*, Appendix, p. 29.
28 *Expositions*, pp. 140–1.
29 Camilla Gray, *The Russian Experiment in Art*, London, 1962, edition revised by Marian Burleigh-Motley, London, 1986, pp. 43–4.
30 Taruskin, *Russian Traditions*, p. 511.
31 Ann Kodicek, 'Sergei Diaghilev' in Kodicek, ed., *Diaghilev: Creator of the Ballets Russes*, London, 1996, pp. 31, 42 and p. 48, n. 32.
32 *Expositions*, p. 141.
33 Letter to N. F. Findeyzen, 2 (15) December 1912, in *Sketches*, Appendix, pp. 32–3.
34 Though written in the first person, the article was in fact ghostwritten by the editor of *Montjoie!*, Ricciotto Canudo. For a full discussion of this much disputed episode see pages 111–13. The text is printed in François Lesure (ed.), *Igor Stravinsky, Le Sacre du printemps, Dossier de Presse*, Geneva, 1980, pp. 13–15.
35 My translation.
36 *Pictures and Documents*, p. 526.
37 The word is Craft's.

2 *Sketches*

1 The reliability of the sketches has been questioned on two grounds. One concerns the order of the sheets, a matter of importance given the changes of direction Stravinsky appears to have made in the course of composition and which are implied by the published order. All one can say is that the pagination, though not by Stravinsky, was believed by him to be correct, and with a few exceptions is supported by the musical evidence. See Craft, 'Commentary to the Sketches' in *Sketches*, Appendix, p. 3, n. 2. Secondly, how complete are the sketches? Suspicions are aroused by the relatively small number for a work of the *Rite*'s scale and complexity; moreover of the 139 published pages a few are blank, others are false starts, and many contain sketches for works other than the *Rite*. Craft's estimate that the collection contains about four-fifths of the original may well be too high (see Robert

Craft, '*The Rite of Spring*: Genesis of a Masterpiece', *Sketches*, p. xv). The only obvious omission is the 'Introduction' to Part I for which nothing has survived beyond one short orchestral draft.

2 Two of the pages were included in Kochno's *Le Ballet en France du XVe siècle à nos jours*, Paris, 1954, pp. 184–5.

3 *Sketches*.

4 See *Sketches*, p. 5.

5 See *Sketches*, p. 104.

6 *Expositions*, p. 147.

7 *Expositions*, p. 141.

8 A letter from Monteux to Stravinsky on 22 February 1913 makes clear that Nijinsky used a two-hand score in rehearsals – see Craft, *Stravinsky: Selected Correspondence*, 3 vols., London, 1984, II, p. 51.

9 *Pictures and Documents*, p. 87.

10 *Montjoie!* 29 May 1913.

11 *Sketches*, Appendix, p. 36.

12 *Montjoie!* 29 May 1913.

13 *Sketches*, Appendix, p. 30.

14 'Divination With Twigs' was Stravinsky's working title for what became 'The Augurs of Spring', of which the 'Dance of the Maidens' forms the second half.

15 *Sketches*, Appendix, p. 30.

16 *Expositions*, p. 141.

17 *Sketches*, pp. 24–5 and 26.

18 Letter to Benois, 2 January 1912, quoted in *Pictures and Documents*, p. 84.

19 The reason given, in a letter from Stravinsky to Benois (26 March 1912) was that 'Fokine is too busy with other ballets, especially Ravel's *Daphnis et Chloë*.' *Pictures and Documents*, p. 85.

20 *Sketches*, Appendix, p. 14.

21 *Sketches*, pp. 46, 50.

22 Craft calls it 'Debussyan' (*Sketches*, Appendix, p. 16).

23 Stravinsky, quoted in *Sketches*, Appendix, p. 14.

24 *Sketches*, p. 54.

25 Dated 7 March. *Sketches*, p. 60.

26 See Taruskin, *Russian Traditions*, p. 954, n. 155.

27 *Sketches*, p. 63.

28 *Sketches*, p. 63.

29 *Sketches*, pp. 66–72.

30 *Sketches*, p. 69.

31 *Sketches*, Appendix, p. 21.

32 *Sketches*, p. 57.
33 *Sketches*, p. 66.
34 *Sketches*, pp. 82–3.
35 *Sketches*, Appendix, pp. 22–3.
36 *Sketches*, p. 64.
37 *Sketches*, Appendix p. 31.
38 When exactly did rehearsals begin? According to Craft, Stravinsky super-
    vised a rehearsal with the dancers in Berlin on 22 November 1912, a mere
    five days after completing the sketch of the 'Sacrificial Dance'. Marie
    Rambert, in her autobiography *Quicksilver*, London, 1972, remembers that
    shortly after she joined the *Ballets Russes* in Budapest, Diaghilev made a
    speech to the company in which he explained the ballet and urged the
    dancers to work faithfully for Nijinsky. This would have been in January
    1913. Stravinsky was summoned to Budapest by an urgent telegram from
    Diaghilev (2 January 1913) – 'Unless you come here immediately for fifteen
    days, the *Sacre* will not take place' (*Pictures and Documents*, p. 93). A letter
    from Stravinsky to Roerich (from Clarens) states that Nijinsky had started
    work on Friday 13 December. Already Stravinsky betrays signs of exasper-
    ation: '. . . he begged me to stay longer. I had to leave but promised that if he
    couldn't manage without my help, I would come to him (for the third
    time!)'. (Quoted in *Pictures and Documents*, p. 92.)
39 Craft, *Glimpses*, p. 314.
40 *Sketches*, p. 84.
41 *Sketches*, Appendix, p. 23.
42 *Sketches*, p. 87.
43 *Sketches*, p. 96.
44 *Sketches*, Appendix, p. 25.
45 The main discussion of 'octatonic' scales is on pages 45–9.

3 Rehearsals and first performance

1 *Pictures and Documents*, p. 83.
2 21 November 1911. See *Pictures and Documents*, p. 83.
3 *Pictures and Documents*, p. 84.
4 *Pictures and Documents*, p. 85.
5 *Pictures and Documents*, p. 85.
6 *Pictures and Documents*, p. 87, from 'Pierre Monteux', *Dance Index*, New
   York, 1948.
7 Doris Monteux, *It's All in the Music: The Life and Works of Pierre Monteux*,

London, 1966, p. 91.
8 Louis Laloy, *La Musique retrouvée*, Paris, 1928, p. 213. This translation from Craft sleevenote.
9 Craft, *Selected Correspondence*, III, p. 4.
10 *Pictures and Documents*, pp. 88–9; see also photo on p. 89 of Nijinsky, Diaghilev and Misia Sert taken by Stravinsky in Venice on 2 (?) September 1912.
11 *La France*, 12 November 1912.
12 Rambert, *Quicksilver*, pp. 58–9. Craft dates this anecdote to the beginning of February 1913, in London – see *Glimpses*, p. 238.
13 *Pictures and Documents*, p. 92.
14 *Pictures and Documents*, p. 93.
15 *Pictures and Documents*, p. 93.
16 *Pictures and Documents*, p. 94.
17 Monteux, *It's All in the Music*, p. 91.
18 Craft, *Selected Correspondence*, II, pp. 52–4.
19 *Pictures and Documents*, p. 97.
20 Sergei Grigoriev, *The Diaghilev Ballet 1909 to 1929*, trans. and ed. Vera Bowen, London, 1953 (1960), p. 93.
21 Buckle, *Nijinsky*, London, 1971, p. 299.
22 Jean Cocteau, *Cock and Harlequin*, trans. Rollo H. Myers, London, 1921, quoted in Buckle, *Nijinsky*, p. 300.
23 Rambert, *Quicksilver*, p. 64.
24 Nijinska, *Early Memoirs*, p. 470.
25 Buckle, *Nijinsky*, p. 300.
26 Buckle, *Nijinsky*, p. 300.
27 Buckle, *Nijinsky*, p. 301 and Nijinska, *Early Memoirs*, p. 470.
28 Stravinsky and Craft, *Conversations with Igor Stravinsky*, London, 1979, p. 46.
29 Monteux, *It's All in the Music*, p. 92.
30 Stravinsky and Craft, *Conversations*, pp. 46–7.

4 Language

1 Stravinsky and Craft, *Memories and Commentaries*, London, 1960, p. 98. According to Taruskin – 'All the fuss connected with this single citation clearly implies that it was the unique instance of its kind in the ballet, tempting one to imagine that Stravinsky made the disclosure expressly so as to create this impression.' Taruskin, *Russian Traditions*, p. 891.

2 Lawrence Morton, 'Footnotes to Stravinsky Studies: "Le Sacre du printemps"', *Tempo*, No. 128, March 1979, pp. 9–16.

3 Taruskin, *Russian Traditions*, p. 893.

4 Taruskin, *Russian Traditions*, p. 900.

5 Rimsky-Korsakov – Sbornik russkikh narodnikh pesen, no. 50: 'Nu-ka, kumushka, mï pokumimsya' (semitskaya). The tune, in Rimsky's arrangement, is quoted in Taruskin, *Russian Traditions*, p. 908.

6 Incidentally, should the 'missing' note (the 3rd of the scale) be G or G♭? My ear hears G♮ – perhaps because of the pattern, and the context (the G naturals at the end of 'Ritual of Abduction'). If G♮, this nicely sets up the G♭ of the dragging E♭ minor chords of 'Spring Rounds' – a switch from major to minor that complements earlier moves from minor to major.

7 *The Nation and Athenaeum*, 18 June 1921, quoted in Lesure, *Le Sacre du printemps, Dossier de Presse*, p. 71.

8 There is a celebrated precedent in Russian music, the music representing the bells from the Coronation Scene of Musorgsky's *Boris Godunov*, whose alternating dominant sevenths, a tritone apart, uncannily foreshadow the sound of the *Rite*.

9 Here, as elsewhere, dominant seventh is used for convenience and without any intention to imply its traditional function in tonal music.

10 Pieter C. van den Toorn, *Stravinsky and The Rite of Spring*, Oxford, 1987, p. 126.

11 *Sketches*, p. 13.

12 Taruskin, *Russian Traditions*, p. 939, n. 140.

13 Taruskin, *Russian Traditions*, pp. 858–9, n. 26.

14 *Sketches*, p. 86.

15 Van den Toorn, *The Rite*, p. 155.

16 Taruskin, *Russian Traditions*, p. 939.

17 See, for example, Taruskin, *Russian Traditions*, pp. 939–40, n. 141.

18 The point receives support from the fact that the *Rite*'s opening dance – 'Augurs of Spring' – is notated in E♭ major. Later, in 'Spring Rounds', Stravinsky notates the music in E♭ minor. The only other instance of a key signature comes in the first eight bars of 'Mystic Circles' (B major).

19 Stravinsky imagined a 'prairie-fire' with the dancers 'rolling like bundles of leaves in the wind'. See *Sketches*, p. xxi.

20 The analogy with film and art is no accident: Pavlova, one of the first stars of the *Ballets Russes* and Nijinsky's first partner in a Diaghilev ballet, was quickly invited to dance and act on celluloid, and Picasso and Braque were both to work with Diaghilev in the coming years. Fokine's choreography, too, worked by drawing the viewer's attention to one or another element at

different times: we 'inspect' the idea of the work as if it were a faceted gem, from different angles, in a way that is entirely familiar to us from television and film but was quite new at the time. See C. Roth, 'Interdisciplinary Parallels: a Study of the Creative Process in certain European Artists, 1880–1914', University of Sheffield Ph.D., 1982, pp. 65–79.

21 The explosive syncopation was one of Stravinsky's most important later inventions. Even in the 1922 full score the pause still comes on the low D. See Louis Cyr, 'Le Sacre du printemps, Petite histoire d'une grande partition', in *Stravinsky: Etudes et témoignages*, ed. François Lesure, Paris, 1982, p. 128.

22 Taruskin's word for this is 'hypostaticized'. Taruskin, *Russian Traditions*, p. 944.

5 *Commentary*

1 'Octatonic' scales are discussed in detail above, Chapter 4 (Harmony).

2 Such 'bitonal' explanations of the *Rite*'s harmony are no longer in favour but in this case are surely right.

3 These have been prefigured in the violas' chord at fig. 12 + 7.

4 See pp. 94 this volume.

5 This represents a change of mind on Stravinsky's part. The sketches show that he originally planned a G♭, subsequently preferring the F because of the G♭ in the next melody, the premonition of 'Spring Rounds' at fig. 28 + 5. See *Sketches*, p. 5, and van den Toorn, *Stravinsky and The Rite*, p. 182.

6 In the sketches this was originally a semitone lower, in the same key as 'Rival Tribes'. In the final score this lower key is preserved in the sudden shocking swerve down a semitone at the clinching repetition (two bars before fig. 44).

7 In the sketches, however, it is clear that the Vivo was composed before the passage at fig. 47.

8 *Sketches*, p. 12.

9 *Sketches*, p. 35.

10 *Sketches*, p. xxi.

11 See Taruskin's detailed examination of 'Dance of the Earth' to which the reader is referred – see Taruskin, *Russian Traditions*, pp. 923–33.

12 *Sketches*, p. 49.

13 Taruskin, *Russian Traditions*, p. 932.

14 Thus I prefer a 'tonal' description of the opening sonority to the octatonic explanation given by van den Toorn, *Stravinsky and The Rite*, p. 165.

15 Considered as a point of departure, the 'push' motif makes an interesting

comparison with the bassoon melody which opens Part I; the difference is that where the Lithuanian melody was a source from which ideas could be quarried, here the basic idea contains the mechanism for its only development.

16 Taruskin, *Russian Traditions*, p. 952.

17 In reality the sketches show that the second tune, being based on a source melody, came first. Incredibly this passage (figs. 93–7) caused Stravinsky more trouble – as far as we know – than anything in the *Rite*, sketches occupying no fewer than eight pages.

18 Translated from the stage directions (in French) in the four-hand score.

19 *Dialogues*, p. 86.

20 *Sketches*, Appendix, p. 14.

21 Taruskin, *Russian Traditions*, p. 958. The bar at fig. 104 + 3 should be conducted not as 9/8, but as four crotchets plus a quaver. Thinking the rhythm in this way gives us the 'added note' which becomes the source of all the relentless irregularity of metre in 'Glorification'. Downbeats arrive with a jolt – as at 105 where the bass note at the end of the previous bar has to be repeated, and again at 107 where the preceding bar is not so much 7/4 as one quaver plus six-and-a-half crotchets!

22 *Sketches*, p. 66.

23 Curiously Stravinsky does not use the convention of dividing bars with dotted verticals, so that the composer can indicate both the sense of the bar and at the same time give practical help to the players. The one exception is the 9/8 bar at fig. 39, in 'Ritual of Abduction', which may be conducted as three dotted-crotchet beats but is to sound as if divided 4 + 5.

24 The D♯ is in collision with not only the high E but also the inner D♮.

25 This desire to place the flute's F on the last beat explains the apparently bizarre barring. This gives precedence to the flute over the trumpets: otherwise the obvious sense of the trumpets' tune would be two bars of 3/2. Through his notation Stravinsky makes clear that the flute is the principal line, the trumpets being a descant.

26 All these are part of the plan. More fortuitous, probably, is the reminiscence in the next bar (fig. 135 + 3), the rhythm recalling the 'fist-shaking' in 'Glorification'.

27 *Sketches*, p. 87.

28 Cecil Gray, *A Survey of Contemporary Music*, London, 1927, p. 143.

29 *Pictures and Documents*, p. 106.

30 *Expositions*, p. 147.

6 *Anthology*

1 Translation by Babette Deutsch and Avraham Yarmolinsky in their *Russian Poetry: An Anthology*, New York, 1972, p. 238.

7 *Stravinsky's collaborators*

1 The other ballets were to music by Debussy (*Prélude à l'après-midi d'un faune* and *Jeux*) and Strauss (*Till Eulenspiegel*).

2 See *Pictures and Documents*, p. 510. The absence of Nijinsky from the stage in a major production of Diaghilev's company is itself noteworthy – it had happened only rarely since he joined the troupe in 1909.

3 *The Diary of Vaslav Nijinsky*, ed. Joan Acocella, trans. Kyril Fitzlyon, Harmondsworth, 1999, pp. 206–7.

4 *An Autobiography*, p. 34.

5 *An Autobiography*, pp. 40–2.

6 *Expositions*, p. 143.

7 John Drummond, *Speaking of Diaghilev*, London, 1997, p.111.

8 *Quicksilver*, p. 68.

9 Rambert's classes were unpopular with the company and earned her the nickname 'rythmichka' (*Quicksilver*, p. 57). No doubt there was an element of jealousy, for she was known to be infatuated with Nijinsky (see Buckle, *Nijinsky*, p. 247).

10 *An Autobiography*, p. 48.

11 *Expositions*, p. 143.

12 See *Glimpses*, pp. 241–2.

13 Drummond, *Diaghilev*, p.111.

14 *Sketches*, Appendix, p. 35.

15 A page of the choreographic notes is reproduced in *Pictures and Documents*, p. 79. In any case we know that Nijinsky worked from a two-hand piano reduction made by Stravinsky. See letter from Monteux to Stravinsky, 22 February 1913, in *Selected Correspondence*, III, p. 51.

16 All this in *Glimpses*, pp. 240–7. See also *Sketches*, Appendix, p. 35, where Stravinsky notes: 'the dance is almost always in counterpoint to the music'.

17 For more about the relationship between Diaghilev and Nijinsky – which may have been platonic rather than sexual – we simply don't know – and the observations of the various women involved as the relationship ended, see Rambert's *Quicksilver* and Buckle's *Diaghilev* and *Nijinsky*.

18 *Sketches*, Appendix, p. 33.

19 LSO/Craft, Koch International Classics, Stravinsky Series Vol. 1.

20 *Pictures and Documents*, p. 512. In the event Nijinsky did choreograph one more work for the *Ballets Russes*, *Till Eulenspiegel*, in 1916.

21 Bronislava Nijinska, *Early Memoirs*, pp. 450–2.

22 Ibid., p 458.

23 *Quicksilver*, pp. 61–2.

24 *Quicksilver*, pp. 61–2. See, however, Lydia Sokolova's description of rehearsals for the *Rite*, *Dancing for Diaghilev*, London, 1960, pp. 42–3.

25 Sokolova, *Dancing for Diaghilev*, p. 163. See also *Pictures and Documents*, p. 509.

26 Massine succeeded Nijinsky as Diaghilev's protégé: he first appeared for *Ballets Russes* in 1914 in *La Légende de Joseph* to music by Richard Strauss with choreography by Mikhail Fokine; both Massine and Fokine were hastily recruited by Diaghilev to fill the different gaps left when Nijinsky married.

27 *The Observer*, 3 July 1921.

28 *Pictures and Documents*, p. 511.

29 *The Observer*, 3 July 1921.

30 'Les Deux "Sacre du Printemps"', *Comœdia Illustré*, 11 December 1920, translation in *Pictures and Documents*, p. 511.

31 *Pictures and Documents*, p. 511.

32 *Pictures and Documents*, p. 511.

33 *Expositions*, p. 144.

34 *Comœdia Illustré* in *Pictures and Documents*, p. 512.

35 See Léonide Massine, *My Life in Ballet*, London, 1969, discussed in *Pictures and Documents*, p. 655, n. 6.

36 *Expositions*, p. 143.

37 Nijinsky's failing mental health reduced him to virtual incapacity during and after the 1916 tour of the Americas; he never really recovered, and ended his days in Virginia Water, Surrey, dying on 8 April 1950.

38 *An Autobiography*, p. 49. Canudo was the dedicatee of a short and (as it happens) extremely Stravinskian piece by Ravel, Frontispice [*sic*].

39 *Pictures and Documents*, p. 523.

40 *Selected Correspondence*, II, p. 104.

41 *Muzyka*, No. 141.

42 *Selected Correspondence*, 1, pp. 54–5.

43 Translation from *Pictures and Documents*, p. 525.

44 See notes from Canudo to Stravinsky (of 22, 26 and 27 May) in *Pictures and Documents*, pp. 522–3. It should be emphasised that Stravinsky enjoyed using words with the same razor-sharp precision as he deployed sounds. When he said the article 'was concocted by a journalist' note that he was

careful not to deny outright his involvement. See *The Nation* (3 August 1980), a letter from Stravinsky in response to an article by Professor Simon Karlinsky (in *Pictures and Documents*, p. 524).

45 Stravinsky and Robert Craft, *Conversations*, p. 94.

46 Nor, for that matter, did Stravinsky ever pay any tribute to the seminal role of Diaghilev.

47 *Sketches*, p. xvii.

48 'The words "For Russian Export" seemed to have been stamped everywhere...' *Expositions*, p. 129.

49 Bronislava Nijinska, *Early Memoirs*, p. 449.

50 Ibid., p. 461.

51 The opening bassoon solo, with its reiterated tracing of a minor key cadence, was perhaps too obvious to be denied. Hence Stravinsky's statement which acknowledged this but nothing else.

52 *Sketches*, Appendix, p. 16.

53 See *Pictures and Documents*, p. 609. The legalities might have been invented by Lewis Carroll. 'Worse still', Craft writes, 'Spencer's melody is not in the *Petrushka* Suite, but since no separate "Suite" was ever published, the non-performance of the twenty-six measures could not be proved.'

54 N. K. Rerikh: Iz literatur-nogo naslediya, p. 361, quoted in Decter, p. 89.

55 Roerich's exaggerated claims about his role in the origins of the *Rite* are discussed by Craft in *Glimpses* pp. 234–6. On p. 247, footnote 1, he writes – 'See the detailed investigation of this monumental con artist in R. C. William's *Russian Art and American Money*, Cambridge, Massachusetts, 1980, and Karl E. Meyer's "The Two Roerichs are One", in the editorial column of The New York Times, 22 January 1988.'

56 *La France*, 4 June 1913, in *Dossier de Presse*, p. 24.

57 *Conversations*, pp. 46–7. See also Buckle, who suggests that Diaghilev deliberately organised the scandal to publicise the *Ballets Russes* season. Buckle, *Diaghilev*, p. 353.

58 *Selected Correspondence*, I, pp. 225–8.

59 *Expositions*, p. 39.

60 *Pictures and Documents*, p. 76.

61 Robert Craft, sleevenotes to *The Rite of Spring*, Koch International Classics.

62 Ibid. See also revised dates of the Paris performances, correcting the account in *Pictures and Documents*, given in *Selected Correspondence*, I, p. 400.

63 See Louis Cyr, 'Le Sacre du Printemps: Petite Histoire d'une grande partition', in *Stravinsky: Etudes et témoignages présentés et réunis par François Lesure*, Paris, 1982, p. 114, n.19.

64 *Sketches*, Appendix, p. 35.

65 The title page of the 1913 four-hand edition says, *Tableaux de la Russie païenne en deux parties d'Igor Strawinsky et Nicolas Roerich*. On the verso of the title page it says, *mise en scène de Igor Strawinsky et Waslaw Nijinsky*. *Choréographie de W. Nijinsky*, *Décors et costumes de Nicolas Roerich*.

66 Stravinsky was not alone. Roerich himself made an interesting comment when recalling the scandal at the first performance. 'Who knows perhaps at that moment they [the audience] were inwardly exultant and expressing their feeling like the most primitive of peoples. But I must say, the wild primitivism had nothing in common with the refined primitivism of our ancestors.' Roerich seems to be saying that the primitivism of the audience had been incited by the primitivism of the music, which was however a distortion of Roerich's vision. See Decter, *Roerich*, p. 20.

67 Lynn Garafola: *Diaghilev's Ballets Russes*, Oxford, 1989, p. 68. Also p. 23 and p. 70.

68 But paradoxically emerging from precisely the same motivation, to embody the 'meaning' of the dance in expressive gesture, whether active or still. Fokine was Nijinsky's teacher, and it shows.

8 *The* Rite *recorded*

1 The suggestion was made in 1912. *Selected Correspondence*, II, p. 5.

2 *Dialogues*, pp. 82–90; Stravinsky and Craft, *Themes and Conclusions*, London, 1972, pp. 234–41.

3 *An Autobiography*, pp. 150–2.

4 For contractual reasons the orchestra on the recording goes under the name of *Orchestre Symphonique*.

5 10 and 18 February 1928. See letter from Craft to Louis Cyr, quoted in the CD booklet, GEMM CD 9334, accompanying Stravinsky's 1929 recording.

6 Louis Cyr gives the date of the Pleyel piano roll version of the *Rite* as 1921. See notes to GEMM CD 9329.

7 The score in question was the 1913 four-hand transcription. One feature of the piano roll is that it includes ornamental passages (printed in small type) which for practical reasons are normally omitted in piano duet performances.

8 Rex Lawson, pianola, Masters MCD 25.

9 See Rex Lawson, 'Stravinsky and the Pianola', *The Pianola Journal*, I, 1987, p. 22. The second part of Rex Lawson's article appears in the second issue of the same journal (II, 1989).

10 '...the essential thing ... [is] ... the pace of the movements and their relationship to one another'. *An Autobiography*, p. 151.

11 The original idea found in the sketches was that 'Spring Rounds' would flow directly out of 'Augurs' at a slightly faster tempo (crotchet = 108 [80]).

12 If the music is reined back at this point, the woodwind tune has a chanting effect which seems to make more apparent its folk music origins. See *Sketches*, p. 7.

13 It seems likely that Monteux recorded his version (with the *Orchestre Symphonique de Paris*) around the time of a concert performance of the *Rite* on 31 May 1929 (see notes by Louis Cyr to GEMM CD 9329). Stravinsky's version was recorded a few weeks earlier – 7–10 May – and stands therefore as the first ever recording of the *Rite* (see notes by Louis Cyr to GEMM CD 9334). Relations between Stravinsky and Monteux were soured by the advertising on behalf of their respective recordings. A press release issued on behalf of Monteux by the *Compagnie Française du Gramophone* stated that it was perhaps thanks to Monteux that the *Rite* was known and not forgotten; that Monteux's interpretation was approved by Stravinsky, and that it was 'the only model on which all conductors base their performances'. Stravinsky's riposte, issued by Columbia Records (France) described his own recording as 'a masterpiece of phonographic realisation ... a model of recording that renders a true service to all those who would like to learn the performance tradition of my work'. *Selected Correspondence*, II, p. 65.

14 *Expositions*, p. 142. Stravinsky's comment is a footnote.

15 The historic (in every sense) account by Monteux for the fiftieth anniversary concert (1963) at the Royal Albert Hall, London, magnificently recreates the old approach, with a hugely exaggerated hold-back (at figs. 174 and 181), the final section (fig. 186) also starting steadily before a marked accelerando.

16 See *Dialogues*, pp. 82–90, and *Themes and Conclusions*, pp. 234–41.

17 A coy transliteration of the Cyrillic script, R. Craft.

18 *Dialogues*, p. 82.

19 *Themes and Conclusions*, p. 234.

20 Ansermet, incidentally, fatally weakens this moment with a gratuitous comma.

21 *Themes and Conclusions*, p. 234.

22 Letter to N. F. Findeyzen, *Sketches*, Appendix, p. 32.

23 See *Dialogues*, p. 83.

24 'This dance is regularly performed too quickly (and lightly and superficially), the composer says.' See Robert Craft, *Sketches*, Appendix, p. 45.

25 'I would notate the strumming at 31 differently today, though I am not certain how,' *Dialogues*, p. 83.

26 *Themes and Conclusions*, p. 235.

27 *Themes and Conclusions*, p. 236.

28 *Dialogues*, p. 84.
29 *Dialogues*, p. 84.
30 As marked in the 1921 score.
31 *Dialogues*, p. 84.
32 Ibid.
33 *Themes and Conclusions*, p. 237.
34 *Dialogues*, p. 85.
35 In Stokowski's later *Fantasia* recording this opening is uniquely slow at crotchet = 33 (48).
36 *Themes and Conclusions*, p. 238.
37 *Themes and Conclusions*, p. 238.
38 *Dialogues*, p. 86.
39 *Themes and Conclusions*, p. 239.
40 *Themes and Conclusions*, p. 239.
41 *Dialogues*, p. 88.
42 *Dialogues*, p. 88.
43 In scores before 1929 there were no such distinctions – see Louis Cyr, *Petite Histoire*, p. 128.
44 See discussion in van den Toorn, *Stravinsky and the Rite*, pp. 52–3.
45 *Themes and Conclusions*, p. 240.
46 *Themes and Conclusions*, p. 240.
47 Louis Cyr, *Petite Histoire*, pp. 94–5.
48 *Seattle Post-Intelligencer*, 5 March 1954, quoted in *Pictures and Documents*, p. 308.
49 *Dialogues*, p. 121.
50 *Themes and Conclusions*, p. 139
51 Conducted by Karajan, Boulez and Craft: *Dialogues*, p. 90.
52 Such indeed may be the case, given the Soviet disapproval of Stravinsky. See also *Dialogues*, p. 89.
53 '. . . the Russians make it sound Russian, which is just right'. *Dialogues*, p. 89.

9 Conclusion

1 Taruskin, *Russian Traditions*, pp. 951–7.
2 Taruskin, *Russian Traditions*, p. 955.
3 Taruskin, *Russian Traditions*, p. 952.
4 Taruskin, *Russian Traditions*, p. 951.
5 Taruskin, *Russian Traditions*, p. 965.
6 Alexander A. Blok, 'Poeziya zagovorov i zaklinaniy in Sobraniye sochineniy v shesti tomakh', V, Izdatel'stvo 'Pravda', Moscow, 1971, pp. 31–59. See also

'Stikhiya i kul'tura', written 1908, pub. 1909.

7 *Memories and Commentaries*, p. 164.

8 *Expositions*, pp. 147–8.

Select discography

The original (British) disc number is given for each recording. Where a second number is quoted, this is the release listened to while working on this book. All these recordings, and many other reissues of these performances, and many other performances of *The Rite of Spring*, both commercial studio performances and live broadcasts, are held in the sound archive of the British Library. 'Digital' indicates that the master recording was digitally encoded.

Piano roll/Rex Lawson (1921)
Recorded 30 September 1990, Dulwich College, London
Innovative Music Productions MCD 25

Walther Straram Concerts Orchestra/Stravinsky (1929)
Recorded in May 1929 at the Théâtre des Champs-Elysées, Paris
Columbia LX 199-23 (5 electrical 12-inch coarse-groove discs)
Pearl GEMM CD 9334 (CD)

Symphony Orchestra/Pierre Monteux (1929)
Recorded in Paris in 1929
HMV W 1016-9 (3 electrical 12-inch coarse-groove discs)
Pearl GEMM CD 9329

Philadelphia Orchestra/Leopold Stokowksi
Recorded in the Academy of Music, Philadelphia on 24 March 1930
HMV D 1919–22 (4 electrical 12-inch coarse-groove discs)
Pearl GEMM CD 9488

New York Philharmonic-Symphony Orchestra/Igor Stravinsky (1940)
Recorded in Carnegie Hall, New York on 4 April 1940
CBS 11367-70D (set M417) (4 electrical 12-inch coarse-groove discs)
Pearl GEMM CDS 9292 (CD)

Philharmonia Orchestra/Igor Markevich (1951)
Recorded in Studio 1, Abbey Road, London on 12 and 13 November 1951

HMV QCLP 12001 (mono LP)
Testament SBT 1076 (CD)

London Symphony Orchestra/Eugene Goossens
Recorded in Walthamstow Assembly Hall, London
Everest LPBR 6047/SDBR 3047 (mono/stereo LP) (released February 1960)
Everest EVC 9002 (CD)

L'Orchestre de la Suisse Romande/Ernest Ansermet
Decca LXT 5388/SXL 2042 (mono/stereo LP) (released 1958)

Columbia Symphony Orchestra/Igor Stravinsky
Recorded in the Ballroom of the St George Hotel, Brooklyn, New York on 5
and 6 January 1960
Philips ABL 3335–6/SABL 174–5 (mono/stereo LPs)
Sony Classical SMK 60011 (CD)

USSR State Symphony Orchestra/Kpaфt (Robert Craft)
Recorded in the Large Hall at the Moscow Conservatory in October 1962
Akkord D-010935-6 (stereo LP)

Berlin Philharmonic Orchestra/Herbert von Karajan
DG LPM 18920/SLPM 138920 (mono/stereo LP) (released 1964)
DG Privilege 4291622 GR (CD)

Orchestre National de la RTF/Pierre Boulez
Recorded on 20 June 1963
Concert Hall CM 2324 (stereo LP)

Cleveland Orchestra/Pierre Boulez
Recorded in Severance Hall, Cleveland on 28 July 1969
CBS 72807 *stereo* in CBS set 79318 (3-LP set)
Sony Classical SMK 64109 (CD)

Los Angeles Philharmonic/Zubin Mehta
Recorded in Royce Hall, University of California, Los Angeles
Decca SXL 6444 (stereo LP) (released 1970)

New England Conservatory Symphony Orchestra/Gunther Schuller
Recorded at the New England Conservatory on 20 October 1971
NEC 108 (stereo LP)

Berlin Philharmonic Orchestra/Herbert von Karajan
Recorded in Philharmonic Hall, Berlin, in December 1975
DG Stereo 2543064 (stereo LP)
DG 415 979-2 (CD)

City of Birmingham Symphony Orchestra/Simon Rattle
Recorded in the Arts Centre, Warwick University, in December 1987
EMI EL 7496361 (stereo LP) *digital*
EMI CDC 7496362 (CD)

London Symphony Orchestra/Kent Nagano
Recorded in the Abbey Road Studios, London, in December 1990
Virgin VMD5 61249 2 (CD) *digital*

London Symphony Orchestra/Robert Craft
Recorded in the Abbey Road Studios, London, in July 1995
Koch International Classics 373592 (CD) *digital*

Bibliography

Acocella, Joan, ed., *The Diary of Vaslav Nijinsky*, trans. Kyril Fitzlyon, Harmondsworth, 1999.

Benois, Alexander, *Reminiscences of the Russian Ballet*, trans. Mary Britnieva, London, 1941.

Blok, Alexander A., 'Poeziya zagovorov i zaklinaniy in Sobraniye sochineniy v shesti tomakh', V, Izdatel'stvo 'Pravda', Moscow, 1971. See also 'Stikhiya i kul'tura', written 1908, pub. 1909.

Boulez, Pierre, *Stocktakings from an Apprenticeship*, trans. Stephen Walsh, Oxford, 1991.

Buckle, Richard, *Nijinsky*, London, 1971.

Nijinsky on Stage: Sketches by Valentine Gross, London, 1971.

Diaghilev, London, 1979.

Cone, Edward T., 'Stravinsky: The Progress of a Method', pp. 155–64 in *Perspectives on Schoenberg and Stravinsky*, ed. Benjamin Boretz and Edward T. Cone, New York, 1972.

Craft, Robert, '*The Rite of Spring*: Genesis of a Masterpiece', *Perspectives of New Music* 5, I, 1966, pp. 20–36 (see also *The Rite of Spring, Sketches 1911–1913*, pp. xv–xxv).

ed., *Stravinsky: Selected Correspondence*, 3 vols., London, 1982, 1984, 1985.

Glimpses of a Life, London, 1992.

Cyr, Louis, 'Le Sacre du Printemps: Petite Histoire d'une grande partition', in *Stravinsky: Etudes et témoignages présentés et révnis par François Lesure*, Paris, 1982.

Decter, Jacqueline, *Nicholas Roerich: The Life and Work of a Russian Master*, London, 1989.

Deutsch, Babette, and Yarmolinsky, Avraham, *Russian Poetry: An Anthology*, New York, 1972.

Drummond, John, *Speaking of Diaghilev*, London, 1997.

Fokine, Mikhail (trans. Vitale Fokine), *Fokine: Memoirs of a Ballet Master*, London, 1961.

Forte, Allen, *The Harmonic Organization of 'The Rite of Spring'*, New Haven, 1978.

Garafola, Lynn, *Diaghilev's Ballets Russes*, London, 1989.

Goossens, Eugene, *Overture and Beginners*, London, 1951.

Gray, Camilla, *The Russian Experiment in Art*, London, 1962, edition revised by Marian Burleigh-Motley, London, 1986.

Gray, Cecil, *A Survey of Contemporary Music*, London, 1927.

Grigoriev, S. L., *The Diaghilev Ballet 1909–1929*, trans. and ed. Vera Bowen, London, 1953 (Harmondsworth, 1960).

Karsavina, Tamara, *Theatre Street*, London, 1930 (1950).

Kerstein, Lincoln, *Nijinsky Dancing*, London, 1975.

Kochno, Boris, *Le Ballet en France du XVe siècle à nos jours*, Paris, 1954.

Diaghilev and the Ballets Russes, New York, 1970.

Kodicek, Ann, ed., *Diaghilev: Creator of the Ballets Russes*, London, 1996.

Laloy, Louis, *La Musique retrouvée*, Paris, 1928.

Lawson, Rex, 'Stravinsky and the Pianola', in *The Pianola Journal*, I, 1987 and II, 1989.

Lederman, Minna, ed., *Stravinsky in the Theatre*, New York, 1949 (1975).

Lesure, François, ed., *Igor Stravinsky, Le Sacre du printemps, Dossier de Presse* [*Press-Book: Anthology of Musical Criticism*], Geneva, 1980.

Macdonald, Nesta, *Diaghilev Observed by Critics in England and the United States 1911–1929*, London, 1975.

Massine, Léonide, *My Life in Ballet*, London, 1969.

Monteux, Doris, *It's All in the Music: The Life and Works of Pierre Monteux*, London, 1966.

Morton, Lawrence, 'Footnotes to Stravinsky Studies: "Le Sacre du Printemps"', *Tempo* 128, 1979, pp. 9–16.

Nijinska, Bronislava, *Early Memoirs*, trans. and ed. Irina Nijinska and Jean Rawlinson, London, 1982.

Nijinsky, Romola, *Nijinsky by his Wife*, London, 1933 (1970).

Rambert, Marie, *Quicksilver: An Autobiography*, London, 1972.

Roth, Colin, 'Interdisciplinary Parallels: A Study of the Creative Process in certain European Artists, 1880–1914', University of Sheffield Ph.D., 1982.

Salmina-Haskell, Larissa, *Russian Paintings and Drawings in the Ashmolean Museum*, Oxford, 1989.

Schæffner, André, *Strawinsky*, Paris, 1931.

Smalley, Roger, 'The Sketchbook of The Rite of Spring', *Tempo* 111, 1970, pp. 2–13.

Sokolova, Lydia, *Dancing for Diaghilev*, ed. Richard Buckle, London, 1960.

Stravinsky, Igor, *An Autobiography*, London, 1975, first published as *Chroniques de ma vie*, Paris, 1935–6, English translation *Chronicle of my Life*, London, 1936.

The Rite of Spring: Sketches 1911–1913, London, 1969.

Stravinsky, Igor, and Craft, Robert, *Expositions and Developments*, London, 1959 (1962).

Conversations with Igor Stravinsky, London, 1979, first published in 1959.

Memories and Commentaries, London, 1960.

Dialogues and a Diary, Garden City, New York, 1963 and London, 1968 (*Dialogues*, London, 1982).

Themes and Conclusions, London, 1972.

Stravinsky, Vera, and Craft, Robert, *Stravinsky in Pictures and Documents*, New York, 1978 (London, 1979).

Stuart, Philip, *Igor Stravinsky: The Composer in the Recording Studio*, London, 1991.

Taruskin, Richard, *Stravinsky and the Russian Traditions*, 2 vols., Oxford, 1996.

Toorn, Pieter C. van den, *Stravinsky and The Rite of Spring*, Oxford, 1987.

Walsh, Stephen, *The Music of Stravinsky*, London, 1988.

White, Eric Walter, *Stravinsky: the Composer and his Works*, London 1966.

Index

Printed in the United Kingdom
by Lightning Source UK Ltd.
107405UKS00001B/73-75